SAP
FOREIGN CURRENCY
REVALUATION

SAP FOREIGN CURRENCY REVALUATION

FAS 52 and GAAP Requirements

SUSANNE FINKE

WILEY

John Wiley & Sons, Inc.

Published by John Wiley & Sons, Inc., Hoboken, New Jersey.

Published simultaneously in Canada.

For general information on our other products and services, or technical support, please contact our Customer Care Department within the United States at 800-762-2974, outside the United States at 317-572-3993, or fax 317-572-4002.

Wiley also publishes its books in a variety of electronic formats. Some content that appears in print may not be available in electronic books.

For more information about Wiley products, visit our Web site at http://www.wiley.com.

Library of Congress Cataloging-in-Publication Data:

Finke, Susanne, 1962–
    SAP foreign currency revaluation: FAS 52 and GAAP requirements / Susanne Finke.
        p. cm.
    Includes index.
    ISBN-13: 978-0-471-78760-0 (cloth)
    ISBN-10: 0-471-78760-4 (cloth)
    1. Foreign exchange—Accounting. 2. Financial statements. I. Title.
    HG3853.7.F565 2006

    657—dc22

Printed in the United States of America

10   9   8   7   6   5   4   3   2   1

To my husband, Kelly, who has always supported and encouraged me through the long hours I've kept on projects and many missed weekends; to my parents, Harry and Grace, who always told me I could do whatever I set my mind to.

CONTENTS

CONTENTS

CONTENTS

PREFACE

This book was written for those in the finance areas of organizations who are responsible for foreign currency revaluation, as well as SAP functional consultants. This book was primarily written for SAP implementations, but the general accounting principles and calculations on currency revaluation are covered in this book and would be beneficial to anyone with or without SAP with foreign currency transactions. The book is divided into three primary sections: statutory requirements, business execution of currency revaluation in SAP, and the configuration of SAP currency revaluation.

Chapter 1 covers the U.S. Accounting statutory requirements, net income, organizational, and financial consolidation impacts. This chapter discusses the Statement of Financial Accounting Standards No. 52 (FAS 52) in high level and provides the link to the official accounting document.

Chapter 2 is an overview of currency revaluation. This chapter briefly discusses stock transfer and tax implications and gives high-level overview examples and a discussion on currency revaluation.

Chapter 3 covers the General Ledger (G/L) Master Data Indicator Impacts. The setup of these G/L indicators, which are usually driven by the business analysts in the finance department, do not normally have corporate standards defined regarding the usage and impact of these settings. This chapter is intended to help define corporate standards for these indicators and explain the impact of these settings on currency revaluation.

Chapter 4 is one of three methods available to run currency revaluation. Currency revaluation without using valuation areas is the way most companies execute revaluation because this was originally the only method available to run revaluation by SAP. This method allows for the posting of revaluation cumulatively, where revaluation and exchange rate difference is calculated each month on the original posting amount, and the same amount is posted to reverse on the first day of the next month. This method also allows for the posting of revaluation incrementally, where revaluation is not reversed each month, and only the incremental difference is posted each month.

Chapter 5 covers one of the newer ways the SAP R/3 software provides to execute currency revaluation. This method requires specific unique configuration that is also covered in this chapter.

Chapter 6 covers a variation of the first and second valuation methods. It uses only one valuation area to execute and is much simpler to implement. This is the preferred method of implementation that most companies are moving toward. This section also requires minimal unique configuration that is covered in this chapter.

Chapter 7 is the "common" configuration to all currency revaluation. Anything specific to a valuation method is covered in the respective chapter. This chapter is placed toward the end of this book, because it is highly technical.

Chapter 8 shows how custom variants can be set up to view the critical fields used in the currency revaluation. The default display for the posting tab used after currency revaluation is complex and includes many unnecessary fields. This view provides a one-page display of the proposed or final postings.

In addition, the Appendix provides some of the commonly used transaction codes (T-Codes) in SAP R/3. The References provide the SAP OSS notes that are noted throughout the book. Finally, the Glossary provides definitions of terms used in the book to provide a common platform for discussion.

Throughout the book, certain important facts appear in grey shaded boxes. These facts are key to assumptions or facts in currency valuation, and special note should be taken if one of these boxes is presented. An example of this is:

> Open Item managed G/L accounts cannot be archived unless they are managed properly and cleared accordingly.

Suggestions for the next version of this SAP book or new topics for SAP books will be received at *info@thesapconnection.com*.

Acknowledgments

I would like to thank my colleagues and clients that have taken the time to endorse this book, Kalpesh Khandhadia, Nadean L. Moore, Dave Paz, and Ron Roberts. I would especially like to thank Ron Roberts, my client at Hollister Incorporated, who took time out of his personal life to read and assist in editing the first drafts of this book.

SAP
FOREIGN CURRENCY
REVALUATION

1

U.S. Accounting Requirements

HIGHLIGHTS

- FASB 52 Requirements Overview
- FASB 52 Currency Exchange Rates
- FASB 52 Currency Translation
- Organizational Impacts

FASB 52: REQUIREMENTS OVERVIEW

The Financial Accounting Standards Board's (FASB) Statement of Financial Accounting Standards 52 (FASB 52), *Foreign Currency Translation*, defines the U.S. generally accepted accounting principles (GAAP) requirements for foreign currency revaluation. The complete Statement can be found on the FASB website *http://www.fasb.org*.

U.S. GAAP requires that Financial Statements be reported in the Functional or Local Currency of each reporting entity. If the Transaction Currency (currency in which the transaction takes place) is not the same as the Local Currency, then the Transaction Currency must be revaluated into the Local Currency using the exchange rate on the key date specified during valuation. The difference between the original posting value and the revaluated amount value results in a financial gain or loss posting on the Financial Statement.

It is important to note that the legal definition of the Country Currency should be represented in SAP as the Local Currency. FASB 52 helps define the legal Local Currency.

When a transaction posting occurs in a currency other than the Local Currency, both the Transaction Currency and the Local Currency get posted on the line item posting in SAP. If a Group Currency (a common reporting currency) is defined, then the Group Currency will be posted along with the Transaction Currency and the Local Currency. The exchange rate used to convert the currencies is that which is in the currency exchange rate table for the postings translation date. This translation date is normally the posting date, but another date may be specified. Assuming these currencies are revaluated on a date different from the translation or posting date, a Gain or Loss (depending on whether the exchange rate goes up or down) will occur and be posted.

FASB 52 requires that revaluation occur on all foreign currency items that are part of an asset or liability period-end balance. Every foreign currency open item is revaluated individually, and the total currency adjustment Gain or Loss is normally posted to a Financial Statement Profit and Loss (P&L) Adjustment Account. In SAP, the account that is being valuated retains its original balance. The balance sheet currency valuation adjustment is posted to a balance sheet account associated with the original account. The original asset or liability account and the balance sheet adjustment account (with the currency adjustment posting) are reported in one item on the Financial Statement. The Gain/Loss posting is reported in Net Income for that period in the Financial Statement unless the transaction hedges a foreign currency commitment or net investment in a foreign entity. In this case, the Gain/Loss is reported in the Cumulative Translation Adjustment (CTA) account in the equity section of the Financial Statement.

FASB 52: CURRENCY EXCHANGE RATES

Paragraph 12 of the FASB 52 (December 1981) states:

> All elements of financial statements shall be translated by using a current exchange rate. For assets and liabilities, the exchange rate at the balance sheet date shall be used. For revenues, expenses, gains, and losses, the exchange rate at the dates on which those elements are recognized shall be used. Because translation at the exchange rates at the dates the numerous revenues, expenses, gains, and losses are recognized is generally impractical, an appropriately weighted average exchange rate for the period may be used to translate those elements.

U.S. ACCOUNTING REQUIREMENTS

Paragraph 27a of FASB 52 (December 1981) states:

Foreign Currency Transactions—The applicable rate at which a particular transaction could be settled at the transaction date shall be used to translate and record the transaction. At a subsequent balance sheet date, the current rate is that rate at which the related receivable or payable could be settled at that date.

The interpretation of this requirement that some companies use is the following:

In order to be in FASB 52 compliance, balance sheet accounts with foreign currency postings (e.g., open payables/receivables) must be revaluated to the Local Currency using the exchange rate in affect as of the balance sheet date. Revaluation is normally run on a period-end basis as part of month-end close using at a minimum an average exchange rate method (spot rates are the preferred method).

P&L Accounts in a foreign currency, represented by revenues, expenses, Gains/Losses will use the spot exchange rate on the date those postings were recognized. If a spot rate is not available the average rate could be used.

If at all possible, use the spot rate when calculating the balance sheet and P&L account currency revaluation (Gain/Loss postings and currency translation from Functional Currency to Group Currency). Adjustments posted to CTA should be recorded similarly. SAP has many transaction codes that allow for updating the foreign currency exchange rates; OC41 is one of them.

> The assumption is made throughout the book that the exchange rate varies from day to day (which it normally does). If, however, it does not fluctuate from the original posting date to the date in which Currency Revaluation is run, there will not be a currency revaluation posting difference.
>
> Because realized exchange rate fluctuations can occur daily, exchange rates should be maintained or updated daily either manually or by an interface such as Bloomberg. It is highly recommended that the exchange rate updates be automated.

FASB 52: CURRENCY TRANSLATION

FASB 52 uses the terms *valuation*, *revaluation*, and *translation* interchangeably. For the purposes of this book, we will use "revaluation" to indicate the revaluation of the Financial Statements from Transaction Currency to Local Currency and "translation" as the Local to Group Currency adjustment process.

If the Reporting Currency of the Financial Statements is different from the Local Currency, then the Financial Statements must be translated from the Local Currency to the Reporting Currency at the exchange rate of the Financial Statement date (normally period-end). This is necessary to report the consolidated Financial Statements of an entire organization in a single currency. This is for internal financial reporting and does not affect the external financial reporting of a company. These translation adjustments are not included in the Net Income, but are reported in a separate component of consolidated equity with the sale or liquidation of the net investment that occurs in a foreign entity.

ORGANIZATION IMPACTS

In order to be in FASB 52 compliance, balance sheet accounts with foreign currency postings must be revaluated to the Local Currency using the exchange rate in effect as of the balance sheet date. Revaluation is normally run on a period-end basis as part of month-end close using at a minimum an average exchange rate method (spot rates are the preferred method). Companies that required consolidated financial statements have different currency revaluation requirements. Companies that produce consolidated financials that have foreign currency postings must translate Local Currency postings into reporting currency. The impact to financial statements is discussed in high level as follows.

Consolidated Financial Statements

Local Currency balance sheets of consolidated foreign subsidiaries are translated according to their functional currency into the Group Reporting Currency at period end using key date exchange rates. The Income Statements are translated at annual average rates. Translation differences of assets and liabilities between the balance sheet and Income Statements do not affect income. They are included in Other Income in the consolidated statements in shareholder's equity. Foreign currency assets and liabilities are translated at period-end closing rates with Gains/Losses reflected in Net Income.

Net Income Impacts

Currency fluctuations that affect cash flows are included in the calculation of Net Income. These would be the Gains and Losses resulting from the revaluation of components of assets or liabilities that originated from foreign currency postings. Gains and Losses resulting from normal short-term or immediate foreign currency intercompany transactions are also included in the Net Income for the period.

Consolidation results should not be included in the Net Income calculation. Long-term intercompany investments in a foreign entity are part of a company's net investment strategy (without immediate Gains or Losses) and should not be included in Net Income. Examples of investments that are not included in the Net Income are demand note payables and advances that are not immediately planned.

2

SAP REVALUATION OVERVIEW

HIGHLIGHTS

- SAP Revaluation Overview
- Stock Transfer Impact
- Tax Impact
- Business Example

There are two different types of revaluation: Revaluation "Type 10," which revalues asset and liability transaction postings to Local Currency, and Revaluation "Type 30," which revalues the asset and liabilities into Group Local Currency by using the difference between the exchange rates.

SAP REVALUATION OVERVIEW

In SAP there are two ways to calculate and post the revaluation "Type 10":

1. Transaction to Local Currency Only
2. Transaction to Local Currency with Group Currency Translation

Unrealized Gain/Loss Posting

Unrealized Gain/Loss postings are a result of the period-end currency revaluation execution. The postings do not become realized until the items are cleared.

The FASB 52 requirements necessitate a revaluation of these open balances (items not cleared) based on the FASB 52 rules. At month-end, currency revaluation should be executed on all foreign currency balances that have not cleared (with the exception of those long-term investments noted earlier). The balances will be revaluated based on the currency exchange rate on the evaluation key date. The differences between the originally translated posting amounts and the revaluation amounts will be posted in SAP as unrealized Gain/Loss postings.

Ways to Run Revaluation

There are three primary ways to configure and run the revaluation. Each will be covered in more detail in its respective chapter. It should be noted that unless business reasons necessitate using process one or two, process three is recommended due to simplicity and compliance with FASB 52 and Group Currency reporting requirements.

1. **Revaluation without valuation areas and no translation, incremental postings.** Revaluation 10 (Transaction Currency to Local Currency) is simply calculated by taking the difference from the current period's valuated balance, less the prior period's valuated balance for Local Currency. There is no accompanying Group Currency translation posting of the Local Currency valuated difference.

    Revaluation 30 (Local Currency to Group Currency) is simply calculated by taking the difference from the current period's valuated balance, less the prior period's valuated balance for Group Currency.

    This can only be posted incrementally without reversals posted. This was the original revaluation created by SAP and is not FASB 52 compliant.

This revaluation method can be executed cumulatively with no reversals taking place. Group Currency translation still does not occur within this variation of execution. It is executed exactly as the incremental method, but the "balance sheet preparation valuation" indicator is not selected in this method, thus the postings are reversed.

2. **Revaluation with valuation areas with translation using full valuation areas.** Revaluation 10 (Transaction Currency to Local Currency) is simply calculated by taking the difference from the current period's valuation, less the prior period's valuation for Local Currency. The additional posting included in this method is that SAP takes the revalued difference in Local Currency and translates that amount to Group Currency. This piece is required for the correct Cumulative Translation Adjustment (CTA) calculation.

   Revaluation 30 (Local Currency to Group Currency) is calculated by taking the current period's valuated Group Currency balance, less the original Group Currency valuated balance, and less the cumulative translation amount in Group Currency (from the revaluation 10 step).

3. **Revaluation with translation using one valuation area.** This is the minimal configuration required to be FASB 52 compliant and still configure the primary account assignment table (V-T030H), as opposed to having to configure the valuation area table (V-T030HB).

   The calculations for this methodology are similar to revaluation using full valuation areas, but the benefits are that only one valuation area is required, and the additional account assignment table does not have to be maintained. The original account assignment table (V-T030H) can still be used. The valuated balance is different from revaluation with full valuation areas, but the calculation results are identical.

[handwritten note in right margin: One we have]

[handwritten note: foreign Currency Valuation same as F06N]

Execution

[handwritten note: ABAP: Execute Program screen]

Transaction code F.05 runs currency revaluation for open items and nonopen items for SAP R/3 4.7. F.06 (used in earlier versions of SAP R/3) is no longer available in 4.7 and will not be discussed here.

It is recommended to execute the program in the background when executing it to create postings in production. Runtimes for cumulative revaluations can be extensive depending on the field selections, the transaction volume, and the method of execution.

Normally, the revaluation is run for all company codes. Business reasons may require running the revaluation for various company codes separately. Some of the driving reasons may be:

- A need to either revaluate one or more General Ledger (G/L) accounts for one company and not others, or to not revaluate one or more G/L accounts for a particular company
- The need to run revaluation daily for some companies and only periodically (like at month-end) for others
- The usage of different valuation methods, possibly utilizing spot exchange rates in one company and average exchange rates in another company
- Company codes that have different fiscal year variants
- Variable usage of Group Currency among company codes
- A decentralized environment with decentralized responsibility for the process or specific G/Ls

Timing

This program should be run on a period-end basis and only once per company code. The program can be executed in test mode as many times as needed. Some companies have requirements to run it daily. It should be run after all period-end posting to Accounts Payable (A/P), Accounts Receivable (A/R), and balance sheet accounts are complete and after period-end clearing is run via F.13. It is recommended to close the period for A/P, A/R, and cash accounts before running F.05, the SAP R/3 valuation program.

> Any type of cumulative revaluation postings can be run multiple times without an indication that revaluation has been run before. It is important to properly track when revaluation is executed.

REALIZED GAIN/LOSS POSTINGS

All foreign currency transaction postings in SAP are immediately translated to Local Currency (and Group Currency where applicable) based on the currency exchange rate from the transaction translation date or posting date (configuration dependent). The Transaction Currency, the Local Currency, and the Group Currency are all entered on the original posting line item in the

BSEG table in SAP. This original posting is never changed by the currency revaluation execution, but is used to compare the revaluated amounts calculated on the key date, with the differences that are posted during revaluation execution.

If the valuation areas are not used in the revaluation method, the valuation differences are posted in the BSEG table for Open Items under the fields BDIFF and BDIFF2. BDIFF stores the results from the last valuation run for the line item transaction to local translation. BDIFF2 stores the results from the last valuation run for the line item transaction to group translation.

If valuation areas are used in the revaluation method, the valuation differences are posted in the BSIS table under the respective valuation area.

When the original posting is cleared in SAP, the realized Gain/Loss posting will be calculated by SAP by calculating the valuation of the original posting using the clearing date and taking the difference from the original posting. The revaluation that was previously run by SAP is already set up to automatically reverse on a particular date set by the revaluation run.

STOCK TRANSFER IMPACT

The G/L account for inventory valuation is determined in the MM configuration (OBYC/KDM). Standard pricing is rarely the same in different company codes with different Local Currencies because of different currency values as well as fluctuating currency exchange rates. These differences are normally posted to either a price difference G/L account or a Gain/Loss G/L account.

During an intercompany posting, there is a "sending" company code, which is normally the shipping point of the inventory. The "receiving" company code is the company code where the inventory is being sent. The following is a brief summary overview of the accounting/business transactions that take place:

- Sending Company Code
  - Credit inventory at standard pricing
  - Debit an intercompany clearing account
- Receiving Company Code
  - Debits inventory
  - Credits an intercompany clearing account

TAX IMPACTS

Tax amounts on foreign currency transactions are normally calculated on the base transaction amount. To enter a different exchange rate (options on how to set or determine it are within the configuration), you have to select this indicator on the global company code configuration (OBY6). Implementing this change results in a Local Currency balance in the document. This balance is posted to another account via configuration under Financial Accounting Global Settings → Tax on Sales and Purchases → Posting → Define Account for Exchange Rate Difference Postings (OBYY).

This indicator is not normally set for U.S. companies. The standard is to leave this blank because issues can arise as a result of the Local Currencies not balancing.

BUSINESS EXAMPLE

The basis for the example is a U.S. company that has a foreign subsidiary in England. The subsidiary in England has a Local Currency in Euros (EUR). The reporting currency of the parent company is the U.S. dollar (USD). The transaction currency in the example is Great Britain Pounds/UK Pound Sterling (GBP).

In Exhibits 2.1, 2.2, 2.3, and 2.4, the English company purchases office supplies on January 5, 2005, for 50,000 GBP. Upon posting the payable in SAP, the 50,000 GBP is immediately valuated into the company's Local Currency (EUR), using the (GBP/EUR) average (M) exchange rate on January 5, 2005. Additionally, Group Currency is posted (EUR/USD). This posting is one line item in SAP with three currencies available for display and reporting (Transaction, Local, Group).

The first revaluation is done on January 31, 2005 (period-end), and the second on February 28, 2005. During each revaluation, the payables in GBP stay the same, but the Income Statement reflects the total revaluated value by means of the adjustment postings resulting during revaluation execution.

Revaluation without Valuation Areas, Incremental Postings

Revaluation 10 (Transaction Currency to Local Currency): Calculated by taking the difference from the current period's valuation, less the prior period's

No Valuation Areas Incremental Postings	Transaction/ Document Currency		Local/ Functional Currency		Group/ Reporting Currency			Exchange Rates	
	Amount	Currency	Amount	Currency	Amount	Currency		GBP/EUR	EUR/USD
5-Jan	50,000.00	GBP	70,525.00	EUR	96,055.05	USD	M-Rate	1.4105	1.36200
31-Jan	50,000.00	GBP	72,105.00	EUR	94,068.18	USD	Spot-Rate	1.4421	1.30460
28-Feb	50,000.00	GBP	72,610.00	EUR	96,193.73	USD	Spot-Rate	1.4522	1.32480

Period 1	Transaction/ Document Currency		Local/ Functional Currency		Group/ Reporting Currency	
	Amount	Currency	Amount	Currency	Amount	Currency
1/31-reval 10	50,000.00	GBP	1,580.00	EUR		
1/31-reval 30	50,000.00	GBP		EUR	−1,986.87	

Period 2	Transaction/ Document Currency		Local/ Functional Currency		Group/ Reporting Currency	
	Amount	Currency	Amount	Currency	Amount	Currency
2/28-reval 10	50,000.00	GBP	505.00	EUR		
2/28-reval 30	50,000.00	GBP		EUR	2,125.55	

Exhibit 2.1   Revaluation without Valuation Areas, Incremental Postings

No Valuation Areas Cumulative Postings	Transaction/Document Currency		Local/Functional Currency		Group/Reporting Currency			Exchange Rates	
	Amount	Currency	Amount	Currency	Amount	Currency		GBP/EUR	EUR/USD
5-Jan	50,000.00	GBP	70,525.00	EUR	96,055.05	USD	M-Rate	1.4105	1.36200
31-Jan	50,000.00	GBP	72,105.00	EUR	94,068.18	USD	Spot-Rate	1.4421	1.30460
28-Feb	50,000.00	GBP	72,610.00	EUR	96,193.73	USD	Spot-Rate	1.4522	1.32480

Period 1	Transaction/Document Currency		Local/Functional Currency		Group/Reporting Currency	
	Amount	Currency	Amount	Currency	Amount	Currency
1/31-reval 10	50,000.00	GBP	1,580.00	EUR		
1/31 valuated bal.	50,000.00	GBP		EUR	92,006.92	USD
1/31-reval 30/CTA	50,000.00	GBP		EUR	−4,048.13	USD

Period 2	Transaction/Document Currency		Local/Functional Currency		Group/Reporting Currency	
	Amount	Currency	Amount	Currency	Amount	Currency
2/28-reval 10	50,000.00	GBP	2,085.00	EUR		
2/28- valuated bal.	50,000.00	GBP		EUR	93,431.52	USD
2/28-reval 30/CTA	50,000.00	GBP		EUR	−2,623.53	USD

Exhibit 2.2 Revaluation without Valuation Areas, Cumulative Postings

14

Multiple Valuation Areas

	Transaction/ Document Currency		Local/ Functional Currency		Group/ Reporting Currency			Exchange Rates	
	Amount	Currency	Amount	Currency	Amount	Currency		GBP/EUR	EUR/USD
5-Jan	50,000.00	GBP	70,525.00	EUR	96,055.05	USD	M-Rate	1.4105	1.36200
31-Jan	50,000.00	GBP	72,105.00	EUR	94,068.18	USD	Spot-Rate	1.4421	1.30460
28-Feb	50,000.00	GBP	72,610.00	EUR	96,193.73	USD	Spot-Rate	1.4522	1.32480

Period 1

	Transaction/ Document Currency		Local/ Functional Currency		Group/ Reporting Currency	
	Amount	Currency	Amount	Currency	Amount	Currency
1/31-reval 10	50,000.00	GBP	1,580.00	EUR	2,061.27	USD
1/31 cum.bal.	50,000.00	GBP		EUR	98,116.32	USD
1/31-CTA	50,000.00	GBP		EUR	-4,048.13	USD

Period 2

	Transaction/ Document Currency		Local/ Functional Currency		Group/ Reporting Currency	
	Amount	Currency	Amount	Currency	Amount	Currency
2/28-reval 10	50,000.00	GBP	2,085.00	EUR	2,762.21	USD
2/28- cum.bal.	50,000.00	GBP		EUR	98,817.26	USD
2/28-CTA	50,000.00	GBP		EUR	-2,623.53	USD

Exhibit 2.3 Revaluation with Multiple Valuation Areas

One Valuation Area	Transaction/Document Currency		Local/Functional Currency		Group/Reporting Currency			Exchange Rates	
	Amount	Currency	Amount	Currency	Amount	Currency		GBP/EUR	EUR/USD
5-Jan	50,000.00	GBP	70,525.00	EUR	96,055.05	USD	M-Rate	1.4105	1.36200
31-Jan	50,000.00	GBP	72,105.00	EUR	94,068.18	USD	Spot-Rate	1.4421	1.30460
28-Feb	50,000.00	GBP	72,610.00	EUR	96,193.73	USD	Spot-Rate	1.4522	1.32480

Period 1	Transaction/Document Currency		Local/Functional Currency		Group/Reporting Currency	
	Amount	Currency	Amount	Currency	Amount	Currency
1/31-reval 10	50,000.00	GBP	1,580.00	EUR	2,061.27	USD
1/31 cum.bal.	50,000.00	GBP		EUR	92,006.92	USD
1/31-CTA	50,000.00	GBP		EUR	-4,048.13	USD

Period 2	Transaction/Document Currency		Local/Functional Currency		Group/Reporting Currency	
	Amount	Currency	Amount	Currency	Amount	Currency
2/28-reval 10	50,000.00	GBP	2,085.00	EUR	2,762.21	USD
2/28- cum.bal.	50,000.00	GBP	2,085.00	EUR	93,431.52	USD
2/28-CTA	50,000.00	GBP		EUR	-2,623.53	USD

Exhibit 2.4 Revaluation with One Valuation Area

valuation for Local Currency. There is no accompanying Group Currency translation posting of the Local Currency valuated difference (see Exhibit 2.1).

Revaluation 30 (Local Currency to Group Currency): Calculated by taking the difference form the current period's valuation, less the prior period's valuation for Group Currency (see Exhibit 2.1).

Revaluation without Valuation Areas, Cumulative Postings

Revaluation 10 (Transaction Currency to Local Currency): Calculated by taking the difference from the current period's valuation, less the original period's valuation for Local Currency (see Exhibit 2.2).

Revaluation 30 (Local Currency to Group Currency) is calculated by taking the original Group Currency amount, adding to it the cumulative translation amount in Group Currency (from the revaluation 10 step), and subtracting the current period's Group Currency calculated amount (see Exhibit 2.2).

Revaluation with Multiple Valuation Areas

Revaluation 10 (Transaction Currency to Local Currency): Calculated by taking the difference from the current period's valuation, less the prior period's valuation for Local Currency. The additional posting included in this method is that SAP takes the revaluated difference in Local Currency and translates that amount to Group Currency. This piece is required for the correct CTA calculation/posting amount (see Exhibit 2.3).

Revaluation 30 (Local Currency to Group Currency): Calculated by taking the Valuated Group Currency Balance ($94,068.18 USD), less the Original Group Currency ($96,055.05 USD), less the Translated Local Currency Adjustment ($2,061.27 USD), using period one as an example (see Exhibit 2.3).

Revaluation with One Valuation Area

Revaluation 10 (Transaction Currency to Local Currency): Calculated by taking the difference from the current period's valuation, less the prior period's valuation for Local Currency. The additional posting included in this method is that SAP takes the revaluated difference in Local Currency and translates that amount to Group Currency. This piece is required for the correct CTA calculation/posting amount (see Exhibit 2.4).

Revaluation 30 (Local Currency to Group Currency): Calculated by taking the Valuated Group Currency Balance ($94,068.18 USD), less the Translated Local Currency Adjustment ($2,061.27 USD), less the Original Group Currency ($96,055.05 USD), using period one as an example (see Exhibit 2.4).

3

G/L ACCOUNT INDICATOR IMPACT

HIGHLIGHTS

- G/L Account Indicator Settings Relevant to Foreign Currency Valuation
- Revaluation Gain/Loss Accounts in Detail
- G/L Account Sample Master Data

The G/L master data indicators can have a significant impact on the outcome of the foreign currency revaluation and translation. The maintenance of these G/L indicators is normally driven by the business analyst in the finance department. Corporate standards are not generally available on these indicators. This section helps set the standards for these indicators by discussing what the impact is to currency revaluation and the impact of changing the indicator after postings have already been made to it. These rules apply to approximately 99% of all situations.

G/L ACCOUNT CURRENCY

The G/L Account Currency defaults to the company code currency when you create a G/L account. If the default of the company code currency is not changed, then the G/L account can accept postings in *any* Transaction Currency. The foreign currency transaction postings will then be translated into Local Currency and to Group Currency for companies managing with Group Currency.

Different Currencies (Company Code and G/L Account Currencies Differ)

If the G/L Account Currency is changed to a currency that is *not* the company code currency, then the G/L account can *only* accept postings in that currency. The only exception to this rule is with foreign currency exchange rate differences. This is commonly used for bank accounts that are maintained in one currency. The foreign currency transaction postings will then be translated into Local Currency and to Group Currency for companies managing with Group Currency.

Same Currencies (Company Code and G/L Account Currencies Are the Same)

The standard setting is the default of the company code or Local Currency unless a company wants to limit postings to a particular foreign currency. Foreign currency bank accounts should be set up this way, identifying the bank G/L account in the foreign currency in which the bank account is managed. The valuation Gain/Loss G/L accounts should have the same currency as their company codes.

Changing the Currency Field Indicator

If you attempt to change the currency from the Company Code/Local Currency or a non-Local Currency to another non-Local Currency (restricting postings to that new currency) after postings have been made, then SAP issues an error message stating that the account has postings and that no change is possible (unless the balance is the new account currency). The balance for currencies that are not the new account currency must be zero, because all relevant evaluations such as interest calculations on the account need to be restricted to the new account currency, and if there is a balance in another currency, this is not possible.

If you attempt to change the currency from any other currency to the Company Code/Local Currency, it is allowed regardless of the account balance. This is allowed because changing it to the Company Code/Local Currency allows any type of currency posting. Therefore, there is no negative effect of this change.

It is recommended that a new G/L account be set up with the correct currency setting and the postings on the old account be transferred to the new account in the desired currency until the old account is a zero balance. The old account should then be blocked for postings.

BALANCES IN LOCAL CURRENCY

Indicator Not Set

If the "Balances in Local Currency" indicator is blank, SAP manages the G/L account balances in Transactional Currency and Local Currency. If the indicator is selected, SAP manages the G/L account balance in Local Currency only. Even if this indicator is set, you can still post foreign currency transactions to this account and they are then translated into Local Currency.

It is recommended not to set this indicator on the following types of accounts:

- Reconciliation accounts (cannot be set)
- Revaluation Gain/Loss accounts
- Foreign Currency revaluation balance sheet accounts
- Accounts not identified to have it set

Indicator Set

If the indicator "Only balances in Local Currency" is set in a G/L account (whether it is an open item or line item account), then the summary tables such as GLT0 (G/L summary table) and ZSPLT (SPL summary table) will contain the Local Currency amount in the Transaction Currency field. The line item databases such as BSEG, BSIS, and BSAS are not impacted by this indicator and will store the original Transaction Currency.

For open item accounts, the currency revaluation program reads table BSEG, or BSIS for open items, so this indicator has no impact on foreign currency revaluation. For line item accounts (non-open item), the currency revaluation program reads table GLT0 for the account balance, so this indicator has an impact for line item accounts on revaluation.

It is recommended to set this indicator for the following types of accounts:

- Cash Discount Clearing accounts (managed on an open item basis)
- GR/IR Clearing accounts

Indicator Impact to Clearing

This indicator impacts the clearing process. If this indicator is set on an open item managed account, it allows those accounts to be cleared in Local Currency without regard to Transaction Currency amounts.

If this indicator is not set on an open item managed account that receives foreign currency postings, the clearing process becomes more complex because exchange rate differences will arise during the clearing process. Separate manual adjustment postings may be required in order to clear these types of accounts.

Balances in Local Currency Field Setting Changes

Changes to this indicator once postings have been made have the same effect as the currency changes. Changes to the indicator cannot be changed unless the account balance is brought to zero. If you attempt to activate the indicator on an account with a balance, SAP will produce an error message.

EXCHANGE RATE DIFFERENCE KEY

This field is used to specify a unique set of accounts when posting Gain/Losses for non–open item managed accounts and nonreconciliation accounts. If the G/L account determination is set up within the open item managed account area for this account (via OBA1), then the Exchange Rate (E/R) difference key is overridden. Most companies leave this field blank. This field can be updated on the G/L account without any impact to revaluation as long as it is configured.

VALUATION GROUP

The Valuation Group indicator is used to group accounts together so the balance can be used to determine the exchange rate type used in the currency revaluation. This field should be left blank on all U.S. company G/L accounts.

OPEN ITEM INDICATOR

The Open Item indicator is normally selected for G/L accounts that require items to be cleared. These accounts need to be cleared at month-end.

Indicator Set

It is recommended to set this indicator for the following types of accounts because subsequent postings can usually be used to clear and offset the original posting:

- Clearing accounts (bank, payroll, goods receipt/invoice receipt (GRIR), etc.)
- Cash Discount accounts

Indicator Not Set

It is recommended not to set this indicator on the following types of accounts because subsequent postings usually do not allow for clearing against the original posting. If there is nothing to be cleared against, the original posting will always remain uncleared.

- Bank Cash accounts
- P&L accounts

- Reconciliation accounts (open item is inherent through its subledger functionality)
- Revaluation Gain/Loss accounts
- Tax accounts
- Raw Material accounts

Open Item Indicator Field Setting Changes

Do not change the G/L account indicator once this account has been revaluated. The correct procedure to make a change to this indicator is to create a new G/L with the correct indicator set, and then perform transfer postings from the old account to the new account. Another approach that may work in most circumstances (but not the recommended approach) is to clear all open items on the G/L in question (zero balance), and then change the indicator.

> Open Item managed G/L accounts cannot be archived unless they are managed properly and cleared accordingly.

LINE ITEM INDICATOR

The Line Item indicator should be selected for G/L accounts managed on an open item basis. This indicator allows you to see the line item postings in reports (FBL3N), rather than just the summary postings. Setting this indicator for all G/L accounts would add a large number of transactional postings to the SAP tables and is not recommended. It is, however, normally selected for most G/L accounts. It does not need to be nor should it be activated for G/L accounts that provide information at the subledger level because this is already at the line item level.

Indicator Not Set

It is recommended not to set this indicator on the following types of accounts because line item detail is available at the subledger level automatically (i.e.,

FLB1N; FBL3N won't be available on the reconciliation G/L unless this indicator is selected, but this is unnecessary).

- Tax accounts
- Receivables Reconciliation accounts
- Payables Reconciliation accounts
- Asset Reconciliation accounts

Line Item Indicator Field Setting Changes

It is possible to change this indicator after postings have been made by first blocking the account, changing the indicator, running program RFSEPA01 (using SE38) to retroactively create line items for documents already posted, and then unblocking the account. Running this program is optional, and if not executed, it will only display line items after the time at which the indicator was activated. The indicator can be deactivated too, but will not result in the deletion of the line item data from the tables. Line item data from the time of change will not be recorded. It is important to note that the correct procedure to change this indicator is to create a new G/L with the correct indicator set, then perform transfer postings from the old account to the new account.

GAIN/LOSS G/L ACCOUNT SETUP

At a minimum, gains and losses should be distinguished using two different G/L accounts, one for gains and one for losses. Ideally, four G/L accounts should be set to track realized gains, realized losses, unrealized gains, and unrealized losses.

The setup of the Gain/Loss G/L accounts should be similar to the indicator status suggested as follows:

- **G/L Currency.** Should be the same as the company code currency.
- **Balances in Local Currency.** Do not set this indicator, because the primary purpose is to revalue items posted in foreign currency.
- **Exchange Rate Difference Key.** Do not set this field.
- **Valuation Group.** Do not set this field.

- **Open Item Indicator.** Do not set this indicator, because these accounts are normally reversed/cleared in the next month.
- **Line Item Indicator.** Set this indicator in order to see the line item postings resulting from revaluation.

BALANCE SHEET OFFSET ACCOUNTS

Except for reconciliation accounts, which cannot accept direct postings, it is not required to set up a different balance sheet account for the currency valuation Gain/Loss offset postings, but it is recommended. Starting in version 4.6, if you use the same balance sheet account as the offset account, you must exclude items that have been revaluated already from the valuation runs. This can be accomplished by either excluding the document type of the revaluation postings (assuming there is a unique document type configured) or by excluding any items whose Transaction Currency is zero dollars.

The setup of the balance sheet offset G/L accounts should be similar to the indicator status suggested as follows:

- **G/L Currency.** Should be the same as the Company Code Currency.
- **Balances in Local Currency.** Do not set this indicator, because the primary purpose is to revalue items posted in foreign currency.
- **Exchange Rate Difference Key.** Do not set this field.
- **Valuation Group.** Do not set this field.
- **Open Item Indicator.** Set this indicator.
- **Line Item Indicator.** Set this indicator in order to see the line item postings resulting from revaluation.

4

REVALUATION WITHOUT VALUATION AREAS

HIGHLIGHTS

- Cumulative Revaluation "Type 10": Period 1 Setup and Execution
- Cumulative Revaluation "Type 30": Period 1 Setup and Execution
- Cumulative Revaluation "Type 10": Period 2 Setup and Execution
- Cumulative Revaluation "Type 30": Period 2 Setup and Execution
- Incremental Revaluation "Type 10": Period 1 Setup and Execution
- Incremental Revaluation "Type 30": Period 1 Setup and Execution
- Incremental Revaluation "Type 10": Period 2 Setup and Execution
- Incremental Revaluation "Type 30": Period 2 Setup and Execution

This method of revaluation revaluates the G/L accounts without using valuation areas and is currently the most common of the methods for revaluation. There are substantial differences in how the Group Currency is calculated between the incremental calculation and the cumulative calculation.

In both the incremental calculation and the cumulative calculation for revaluation 10 (Transaction Currency to Local Currency), the valuation posted is simply the difference of the Local Currency between periods. Incremental calculation takes the difference between the current period and the prior period, whereas the cumulative calculation takes the difference between the current period and the original posting.

Revaluation 30 (Local Currency to Group Currency) for the incremental method is simply the difference of the Group Currency for the current period and the Group Currency for the prior period.

	Transaction is Accessed via:
Via Menus	Accounting → Financial Accounting → General Ledger → Periodic Processing → Closing → Valuate → Foreign Currency Valuation (Exhibit 4.2)
Via Transaction Code	F.05

Exhibit 4.1   Access Sequence

Revaluation 30 (Local Currency to Group Currency) for the cumulative method is the difference of the EUR/USD exchange rates for the current period and the original period, times the original Local Currency posting in EUR to obtain USD.

These methods are not FASB 52 compliant because they do not translate the Local Currency Gain/Loss to Group Currency.

SAP provides a means to execute foreign currency revaluation on specific G/L accounts managed in foreign currencies. Exhibit 4.1 describes the menu path and transaction code, and Exhibit 4.2 shows it on the menu. Transaction code F.05 allows the revaluation of one or more accounts at the same time. The following steps occur with currency revaluation execution:

Exhibit 4.2   Menu Path

Step 1. Each G/L account's line item selected is revalued using the exchange rate of the key evaluation date.

Step 2. A posting is generated to the appropriate unrealized Gain/Loss account and balance statement adjustment account.

Step 3. Postings can be incremental with no reversals posted or cumulative with reversals posted.

Currency revaluation has various configurations that are required:

- Exchange rate types are set up.
- Valuation methods are set up (OB59).
- Document types are set up (OBA7).
- Exchange rates are entered for each currency (OC41).
- Account determination has been defined (OBA1).
- Posting keys are assigned for adjustment postings.

CUMULATIVE REVALUATION "TYPE 10": PERIOD 1 SETUP AND EXECUTION 1/31/2005

In this section, the foreign currency account balances will be revaluated by converting the Transaction Currency posting (GBP) to Local Currency (EUR) using the exchange rate for the original posting, and the Transaction Currency posting (GBP) to Local Currency (EUR) using the exchange rate for the evaluation key date. The difference that results from the exchange rate fluctuations on the date of revaluation will be posted in SAP.

Header Data

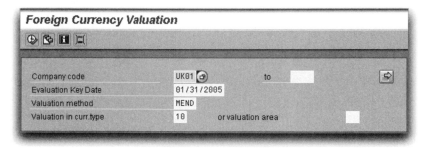

© SAP AG, 2006

- **Company Code.** Select the company code or company codes that are to be revaluated. Some companies prefer to centralize this function, whereas other companies decentralize it. Either way, you can run it for one or more company codes at the same time. It depends on how you want to analyze the output.

> When you run this for multiple company codes, the G/L accounts that are selected for revaluation are run for all companies selected. For example, a specific G/L account (e.g., 2050) might exist in all company codes, but revaluation runs might only be desired in one or a select number of company codes. If company codes have different G/Ls that require revaluation, it might be best to run the company codes individually.

- **Evaluation Key Date.** The evaluation key date is used to determine the date of the currency exchange rates used in the revaluation. SAP will look for the exchange rate that falls on the key date entered. If one does not exist for that specific date, it will look for the exchange rate for the closest date prior to the date entered as the evaluation key date. The evaluation key date should be the last day of the period.

  The evaluation key date is also used to evaluate open item documents that have not been cleared as of this date (period 13 through period 16 are considered if the key date is within periods 1 through 12).

- **Valuation Method.** Valuation method is the key that determines a foreign currency valuation method/approach used when carrying out the foreign currency revaluation. The most important field read from the valuation method is the type of exchange rate used (average or spot). Refer to the common configuration area to read more information specific to this key.

- **Valuation in Currency Type or Valuation Area.** Valuation currency type defines the type of valuation being performed. First local currency type defined for valuation defines the Currency Type for Transactional Currency to Local Currency valuation ("Type 10" in these examples).

Postings Tab

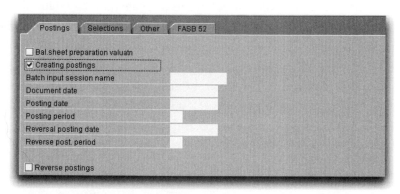

© SAP AG, 2006

- **Balance Sheet Preparation Valuation.** This parameter can only be used for valuation runs that do not use valuation areas. This indicator does not have an effect on non–open item accounts; it only affects open item accounts.

  For open item accounts, this indicator is key. If *not* selected, reversals will be posted and valuation will be cumulative. If selected, no reversal postings will occur and valuation will be incremental. Refer to SAP Note No. 87538 in the References section at the end of the book. Most companies that run revaluation via this method (e.g., not using valuation areas) do not reverse postings and post incrementally.

  To post reversals for non–open item accounts, select the "reverse postings" indicator at the bottom under "For G/L Account Balance Valuation" and choose a date. To post reversals for both open item and non–open item accounts, do not select the balance sheet preparation valuation indicator and select the reverse postings indicator at the bottom.

- **Create Postings.** Leave this indicator blank to run the valuation in test mode. Select the indicator to make the postings in Finance (FI). When selected, the postings can either be executed immediately in the foreground, in the background, or a batch input session can be specified.

- **Batch Input Session Name.** If you enter a name here, a batch input session with that name will be created. Transaction SM35 must be used to process the batch session. The postings will not be made until the batch session is processed. If you do not enter a name here, the postings will be made immediately.

- **Document Date.** The document date of the unrealized postings can be specified here or SAP will default to the valuation key date.
- **Posting Date.** The posting date of the unrealized postings can be specified here or SAP will default to the valuation key date.
- **Posting Period.** Posting period in which the valuation postings are generated. The number entered should correspond to the period that includes the posting date or valuation key date.
- **Reversal Posting Date.** The posting date of the reversal postings can be specified here; otherwise, SAP will default to the next day. This is normally the first day of the next period or the next day if running valuation daily. This is for non–open item accounts only.
- **Reversal Posting Period.** This is the posting period in which the valuation postings are generated. This must correspond to the posting date. This is for non–open item accounts only.
- **Reverse Postings.** This indicator affects the valuation of non–open items only. If not selected, the G/L balances for non–open item accounts will not be reversed. If selected, they will be reversed in full.

Selections Tab

- **Valuate G/L Account Open Items.** Select this indicator in combination with identifying the specific open item G/L accounts to be valuated.

- **Valuate G/L Account Balances.** Select this indicator in combination with identifying the specific G/L balance accounts to be valuated.

- **G/L Account.** Identify the specific open item G/L account(s) that will be revaluated. These same G/L accounts will appear in the G/L balance tab, and even if the "Valuate G/L Account Open Items" indicator is selected, the accounts identified in both the open items and G/L balance tab will be valuated based on their G/L account definition as open item or line item. If a range of G/L accounts that include both open item and non–open item accounts is identified, and only the "Valuate G/L Account Open Items" indicator is selected, then only the G/L accounts in the range that are open item will be revaluated.

- **No GR/IR Accounts.** If selected, no GR/IR valuation will occur. GR/IR should be revaluated.

- **Evaluate GR/IR Accounts.** If selected, open items with a goods receipt (MIGO) will be valuated in the GR/IR account. The Purchase Order Currency is then valuated. The valuation is only completed if the goods receipt has occurred, because this is when the first financial posting occurs. The GR/IR account is an open item account, and postings will automatically be reversed. Revaluation occurs based on the Purchase Order Currency. Refer to SAP Note No. 441333 in the References for more information.

- **GR/IR with FI Data.** If you select this indicator, revaluation will occur on *all* items in the GR/IR account. U.S. clients may choose to use this field as opposed to the previous field because this gives more control to the person running the revaluation.

- **GR/IR Delivery Costs.** Specify accounts for GR/IR transaction cost postings. Transactions with debit balances (invoices without goods) should not be valuated. The vendor invoice will be valuated. Goods delivered but not invoiced will be valuated with this indicator setting.

- **Valuate P&L Accounts.** Select to valuate P&L accounts. This is not normally selected unless fixed asset depreciation is being revaluated. Do not reverse P&L postings.

- **Valuate Period Balance Only.** This is not normally selected unless running revaluation on P&L accounts. Selecting this indicator valuates the period balance and not the cumulative balance.

- **Exchange Rate Difference Key.** If exchange rate difference keys are utilized on G/L account master data for non–open item accounts, this field can be used to uniquely identify the valuation for specific exchange rate keys.

- **Business Area.** Revaluation can be run for specific business areas (if business areas are used).

- **Valuate Vendor Open Items.** To valuate vendor (payables) open items, select this indicator and select the appropriate vendors or range of vendors in the next field.

- **Vendor.** Select the vendor(s) or range of vendors to valuate along with the previous indicator "Value Vendor Open Items."

- **Valuate Customer Open Items.** To valuate customer (receivable) open items, select this indicator and select the appropriate customers or range of customers in the next field.

- **Customer.** Select the customer(s) or range of customers to valuate, along with the previous indicator "Valuate Customer Open Items."

- **Reconciliation Account.** This field can be used as an alternative to listing the vendors or customers. The vendor or customer reconciliation accounts are listed here. If used, only vendors (or customers) assigned to this G/L reconciliation account(s) will be valuated.

- **Document Number.** This is used to select one or more specific documents for valuation. This is not normally used for production runs but is useful in testing valuation so that valuation and postings are kept to a specific document test.

- **Currency.** Valuation runs can be limited to execution by currency. To run revaluation on just GBP currency, enter this. Leaving this field blank will select all open items for valuation for any currency.

- **SL Extra.** Split ledger (SL) functionality in SAP R/3 v4.7 allows you to distribute valuation differences to profit centers or business areas based on how the split ledger ZZPLIT is set up.

Other Tab

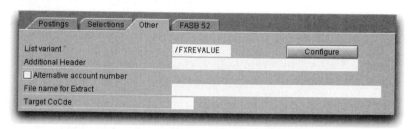

- **List Variant.** The list variant is useful in displaying all of the balances SAP uses to calculate the valuation postings.

- **Additional Header.** A report header/description can be entered here, and it will be entered on the valuation report.

- **Alternative Account Number.** If selected, the alternative account number defined on the G/L account master record is used. This is normally used if a country chart of accounts is maintained in the company codes selected. Remember that the financial statements will need to be updated to include the alternative accounts. Normally, this is not selected.

- **File Name for Extract.** Enter a file name if an extract is desired. Otherwise, leave this field blank.

- **Target Co-code.** A cross-company code can be entered for the valuation postings. Normally, this is left blank.

FASB 52 Tab

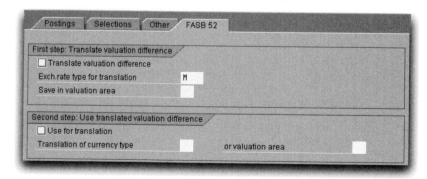

- **Translate Valuation Difference.** Select this indicator to execute the translation using valuation areas. This is not used without valuation areas.

- **Exchange Rate Type for Translation.** Select the appropriate exchange rate type. This is not used without valuation areas.

- **Save in Valuation Area.** Select a valuation area to store the valuation in this field. This is not used without valuation areas.

- **Use for Translation.** This is not used for revaluation "Type 10" (Transaction to Local Currency). This is used for the second step, revaluation 30 (Transaction to Group Currency). This is not used without valuation areas.

- **Translation of Currency Type or Valuation Area.** This is not used for revaluation "Type 10" (Transaction to Local Currency). This is used for the second step, revaluation 30 (Transaction to Group Currency). This is not used without valuation areas.

SAP Execution: Execution

Key date 01/31/05
Valuation in Company code currency (10)
Method MEND Month End Valuation Method

G/L acct	Amount in FC	Curr.	Amt. in loc.cur.	Amount valuated	Exch.rate	Exch.rate	Ty	Pstg date	Old difference	New difference
140000	50,000.00	GBP	70,525.00	72,105.00	1.4210	1.41050	KR	01/05/2005	0.00	1,580.00
* 140000		GBP	70,525.00						0.00	1,580.00
** 140000			70,525.00						0.00	1,580.00
*** Target Comp. Code UK01			70,525.00						0.00	1,580.00

- **Amount in FC.** This is the document currency (50,000 GBP in this example).

- **Amount in Local Currency.** This is the open item cumulative balance in Local Currency (70,525.00 EUR in this example).

- **Amount Valuated.** This is the Transaction Currency (50,000 GBP) translated into Local Currency (72,105.00 EUR) on the key date.

- **Old Difference.** This is the cumulative valuation adjustment that resulted from the prior valuation.

- **New Difference.** This is the current cumulative valuation adjustment, which is the valuated amount, Transaction Currency translated into EUR on the key date (72,105.00 EUR), less the Local Currency amount in EUR (70,525.00 EUR).

SAP Execution: Postings

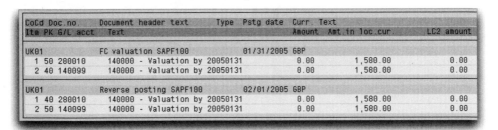

© SAP AG, 2006

- **Amount in Local Currency.** This is the difference between the new valuated amount (72,105.00 EUR) and the old valuated amount (70,525.00 EUR).

- **Local Currency 2 Amount.** This is the Local Currency (EUR) revaluated difference translated into Group Currency (USD). This is not executed or posted with this process method.

- **Process Batch Session.** If a batch session was created, run transaction SM35 to process the batch session. Select "Process errors only," and Execute.

SAP Execution: Validation

In order to validate the results, select a few G/L accounts to analyze. Use the following steps to compare the revaluation from Transaction to Local Currency:

Step 1. Run SAP transaction code FBL3N for the open items on the key date for the same G/L accounts selected, or select a few to review. Exclude the amounts (Transaction Currency) where they are zero so you do not pick up adjustment amounts. Take the Transaction Currency and convert it to the Local Currency using the exchange rate for the key date being used.

Step 2. Take the original Local Currency (prior period) and the Local Currency amount calculated by the previous step and compare the SAP calculation, Exhibit 4.3.

No Valuation Areas Cumulative Postings	Transaction/ Document Currency		Local/ Functional Currency		Group/ Reporting Currency			Exchange Rates	
	Amount	Currency	Amount	Currency	Amount	Currency		GBP/EUR	EUR/USD
5-Jan	50,000.00	GBP	70,525.00	EUR	96,055.05	USD	M-Rate	1.4105	1.36200
31-Jan	50,000.00	GBP	72,105.00	EUR	94,068.18	USD	Spot-Rate	1.4421	1.30460
28-Feb	50,000.00	GBP	72,610.00	EUR	96,193.73	USD	Spot-Rate	1.4522	1.32480

Period 1	Transaction/ Document Currency		Local/ Functional Currency		Group/ Reporting Currency	
	Amount	Currency	Amount	Currency	Amount	Currency
1/31-reval 10	50,000.00	GBP	1,580.00	EUR		

Exhibit 4.3 Excel Calculation

CUMULATIVE REVALUATION "TYPE 30": PERIOD 1 SETUP AND EXECUTION 1/31/2005

In this section, the foreign currency account balances will be revaluated by taking the difference of the EUR/USD exchange rate for the current period and the original period, times the original Local Currency posting. The difference that results from the exchange rate fluctuations on the date of revaluation will be posted in SAP.

Header Information

© SAP AG, 2006

- **Company Code.** Select the company code or codes that are to be revaluated. Some companies prefer to centralize this function, whereas others decentralize it. Either way, you can run it for one or more company codes at the same time. It depends on how you want to analyze the output.

> When you run this for multiple company codes, the G/L accounts that are selected for revaluation are run for all companies selected. For example, a specific G/L account (e.g., 2050) might exist in all company codes, but revaluation runs might only be desired for one or a select number of company codes. If company codes have different G/Ls that require revaluation, it might be best to run the company codes individually.

- **Evaluation Key Date.** The evaluation key date is used to determine the date of the Currency Exchange Rates used in the revaluation. SAP will look for the exchange rate that falls on the key date entered. If one doesn't exist for that specific date, it will look for the exchange rate for the closest date prior to the date entered as the evaluation key date. The evaluation key date should be the last day of the period.

The evaluation key date is also used to evaluate open item documents that have not been cleared as of this date (period 13 through period 16 are considered if the key date is within periods 1 through period 12).

- **Valuation Method.** Valuation method is the key that determines a foreign currency valuation method/approach used when carrying out the foreign currency revaluation. The most important field read from the valuation method is the type of exchange rate used (average or spot). Refer to the common configuration area to read more information specific to this key.

- **Valuation in Currency Type or Valuation Area.** Valuation currency type defines the type of valuation being performed. Second Local Currency type defined for valuation defines the Currency Type for Local Currency to Group Currency valuation ("Type 30" in these examples).

Postings Tab

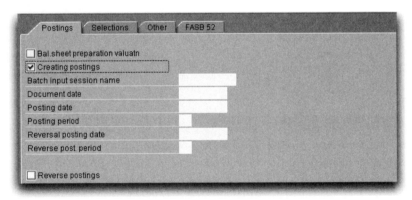

© SAP AG, 2006

- **Balance Sheet Preparation Valuation.** This parameter can only be used for valuation runs that do not use valuation areas. This indicator does not have an effect on non–open item accounts; it only affects open item accounts.

For open item accounts, this indicator is key. If *not* selected, reversals will be posted and valuation will be cumulative. If selected, no reversal postings will occur and valuation will be incremental. Refer to

SAP Note No. 87538 in the References. Most companies that run revaluation via this method (e.g., not using valuation areas) do not reverse postings and post incrementally.

To post reversals for non–open item accounts, select the "reverse postings" indicator at the bottom under "For G/L Account Balance Valuation" and choose a date. To post reversals for both open item and non–open item accounts, do not select the balance sheet preparation valuation indicator and select the reverse postings indicator at the bottom.

- **Create Postings.** Leave this indicator blank to run the valuation in test mode. Select the indicator to make the postings in FI. When selected, the postings can either be executed immediately in the foreground, in the background, or a batch input session can be specified.

- **Batch Input Session Name.** If you enter a name here, a batch input session with that name will be created. Transaction SM35 must be used to process the batch session. The postings will not be made until the batch session is processed. If you do not enter a name here, the postings will be made immediately.

- **Document Date.** The document date of the unrealized postings can be specified here or SAP will default to the valuation key date.

- **Posting Date.** The posting date of the unrealized postings can be specified here or SAP will default to the valuation key date.

- **Posting Period.** Posting period in which the valuation postings are generated. The number entered should correspond to the period that includes the posting date or valuation key date.

- **Reversal Posting Date.** The posting date of the reversal postings can be specified here; otherwise, SAP will default to the next day. This is normally the first day of the next period or the next day if running valuation daily. This is for non–open item accounts only.

- **Reversal Posting Period.** This is the posting period in which the valuation postings are generated. This must correspond to the posting date. This is for non–open item accounts only.

- **Reverse Postings.** This indicator affects the valuation of non–open items only. If not selected, the G/L balances for non–open item accounts will not be reversed. If selected, they will be reversed in full.

Selections Tab

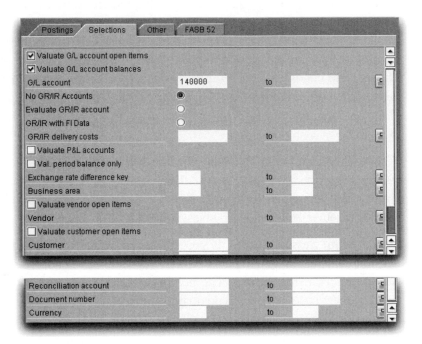

© SAP AG, 2006

- **Valuate G/L Account Open Items.** Select this indicator in combination with identifying the specific open item G/L accounts to be valuated.

- **Valuate G/L Account Balances.** Select this indicator in combination with identifying the specific G/L balance accounts to be valuated.

- **G/L Account.** Identify the specific open item G/L account(s) that will be revaluated. These same G/L accounts will appear in the G/L balance tab, and even if the "Valuate G/L Account Open Items" indicator is selected, the accounts identified in both the open items and G/L balance tab will be valuated based on their G/L account definition as open item or line item. If a range of G/L accounts that include both open item and non–open item accounts is identified, and only the "Valuate G/L Account Open Items" is selected, then only the G/L accounts in the range that are open item will be revaluated.

- **No GR/IR Accounts.** If selected, no GR/IR valuation will occur. GR/IR should be revaluated.

- **Evaluate GR/IR Accounts.** If selected, open items with a goods receipt (MIGO) will be valuated in the GR/IR account. The Purchase Order Currency is then valuated. The valuation is only completed if the goods receipt has occurred, because this is when the first financial posting occurs. The GR/IR account is an open item account, and postings will automatically be reversed. Revaluation occurs based on the Purchase Order Currency. Refer to SAP Note No. 441333 in the References for more information.

- **GR/IR with FI Data.** If you select this indicator, revaluation will occur on *all* items in the GR/IR account. U.S. clients may choose to use this field as opposed to the previous field because this gives more control to the person running the revaluation.

- **GR/IR Delivery Costs.** Specify accounts for GR/IR transaction cost postings. Transactions with debit balances (invoices without goods) should not be valuated. The vendor invoice will be valuated. Goods delivered but not invoiced will be valuated with this indicator setting.

- **Valuate P&L Accounts.** Select to valuate P&L accounts. This is not normally selected unless fixed asset depreciation is being revaluated. Do not reverse P&L postings.

- **Valuate Period Balance Only.** This is not normally selected unless running revaluation on P&L accounts. Selecting this indicator valuates the period balance and not the cumulative balance.

- **Exchange Rate Difference Key.** If exchange rate difference keys are utilized on G/L account master data for non-open item accounts, this field can be used to uniquely identify the valuation for specific exchange rate keys.

- **Business Area.** Revaluation can be run for specific business areas (if business areas are used).

- **Valuate Vendor Open Items.** To valuate vendor (payables) open items, select this indicator and select the appropriate vendors or range of vendors in the next field.

- **Vendor.** Select the vendor(s) or range of vendors to valuate along with the previous indicator "Value Vendor Open Items."

- **Valuate Customer Open Items.** To valuate customer (receivable) open items, select this indicator and select the appropriate customers or range of customers in the next field.

- **Customer.** Select the customer(s) or range of customers to valuate, along with the previous indicator "Valuate Customer Open Items."

- **Reconciliation Account.** This field can be used as an alternative to listing the vendors or customers. The vendor or customer reconciliation accounts are listed here. If used, only vendors (or customers) assigned to this G/L reconciliation account(s) will be valuated.

- **Document Number.** This is used to select one or more specific documents for valuation. This is not normally used for production runs but is useful in testing valuation so that valuation and postings are kept to a specific document test.

- **Currency.** Valuations runs can be limited to execution by currency. To run revaluation on just GBP currency, enter this indicator. Leaving this field blank will select all open items for valuation for any currency.

- **SL Extra.** Split ledger functionality in SAP R/3 v4.7 allows you to distribute valuation differences to profit centers or business areas based on how the split ledger ZZPLIT is set up.

Other Tab

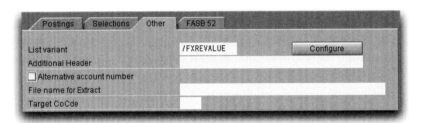

© SAP AG, 2006

- **List Variant.** The list variant is useful in displaying all of the balances SAP uses to calculate the valuation postings.

- **Additional Header.** A report header/description can be entered here, and it will be entered on the valuation report.

- **Alternative Account Number.** If selected, the alternative account number defined on the G/L account master record is used. This is normally used if a country chart of accounts is maintained in the company codes selected. Remember that the financial statements will need to be updated to include the alternative accounts. Normally, this is not selected.

- **File Name for Extract.** Enter a file name if an extract is desired. Otherwise, leave this field blank.

- **Target Co-code.** A cross-company code can be entered for the valuation postings. Normally, this is left blank.

FASB 52 Tab

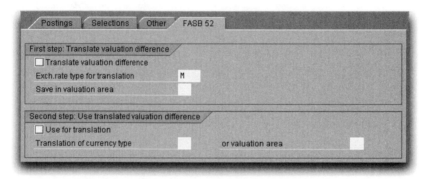

© SAP AG, 2006

- **Translate Valuation Difference.** Select this indicator to execute the translation using valuation areas. This is not used without valuation areas.

- **Exchange Rate Type for Translation.** Select the appropriate exchange rate type. This is not used without valuation areas.

- **Save in Valuation Area.** Select a valuation area to store the valuation in this field. This is not used without valuation areas.

- **Use for Translation.** This is not used for revaluation "Type 10" (Transaction to Local Currency). This is used for the second step, revaluation 30 (Transaction to Group Currency). This is not used without valuation areas.

- **Translation of Currency Type or Valuation Area.** This is not used for revaluation "Type 10" (Transaction to Local Currency). This is used for the second step, revaluation 30 (Transaction to Group Currency). This is not used without valuation areas.

SAP Execution: Execution

Key date 01/31/05
Valuation in Group currency (30)
Method MEND Month End Valuation Method

G/L acct	Amount in FC	Curr	Amount grp curr	Amount valuated	Exch.rate	Exch.rate	Ty	Pstg date	Old difference	New difference
140000	70,525.00	EUR	96,055.05	92,006.92	1.30460	1.36200	KR	01/05/2005	0.00	4,048.13-
140000		EUR	96,055.05						0.00	4,048.13-
* 140000			96,055.05						0.00	4,048.13-
*** Target Comp. Code UK01			96,055.05						0.00	4,048.13-

- **Amount in FC.** For group valuation, this is the Local Currency amount in EUR (open item cumulative balance) from the valuation "Type 10" calculation (70,525 EUR in this example).

- **Amount in Group Currency.** This is the open item cumulative balance in Group Currency ($96,055.05 USD in this example)

- **Amount Valuated.** This is the Group Currency on the key date ($94,068.18 USD), less the Local Currency valuation (1,580 EUR), translated into Group Currency $2,061.27 (USD) on key date ($92,006.92 USD in this example).

- **Old Difference.** This is the cumulative valuation adjustment that resulted from the most recent valuation.

- **New Difference.** This is the current cumulative valuation adjustment, which is the valuated amount ($92,006.92 USD) less the original Group Currency amount ($96,055.05 USD).

SAP Execution: Posting

CoCd Doc.no.	Document header text	Type	Pstg date	Curr. Text		
Itm PK G/L acct	Text			Amount	Amt.in loc.cur.	LC2 amount
UK01	FC valuation SAPF100		01/31/2005	GBP		
1 40 230010	140000 - Valuation by 20050131			0.00	0.00	4,048.13
2 50 140099	140000 - Valuation by 20050131			0.00	0.00	4,048.13
UK01	Reverse posting SAPF100		02/01/2005	GBP		
1 50 230010	140000 - Valuation by 20050131			0.00	0.00	4,048.13
2 40 140099	140000 - Valuation by 20050131			0.00	0.00	4,048.13

- **Local Currency Amount.** This is not relevant in this valuation method "Type 30."

- **Local Currency 2 Amount.** This is the current amount valuated ($92,006.92 USD) less the original Group Currency amount ($96,055.05 USD).

- **Process Batch Session.** If a batch session was created, run transaction SM35 to process the batch session. Select "Process errors only," and Execute.

SAP Execution: Validation

In order to validate the results, select a few G/L accounts to analyze. Use the following steps to compare the revaluation from Transaction to Local Currency:

- Run SAP transaction code FBL3N for the open items on the key date for the same G/L accounts selected, or select a few to review. Exclude the amounts (Transaction Currency) where they are zero so you do not pick up adjustment amounts. Take the Transaction Currency and convert it to the Local Currency using the exchange rate for the key date being used.

- Take the original Local Currency (prior period) and the Local Currency amount calculated by the previous step and compare the SAP calculation, Exhibit 4.4.

No Valuation Areas Cumulative Postings	Transaction/Document Currency		Local/Functional Currency		Group/Reporting Currency			Exchange Rates	
	Amount	Currency	Amount	Currency	Amount	Currency		GBP/EUR	EUR/USD
5-Jan	50,000.00	GBP	70,525.00	EUR	96,055.05	USD	M-Rate	1.4105	1.36200
31-Jan	50,000.00	GBP	72,105.00	EUR	94,068.18	USD	Spot-Rate	1.4421	1.30460
28-Feb	50,000.00	GBP	72,610.00	EUR	96,193.73	USD	Spot-Rate	1.4522	1.32480

Period 1	Transaction/Document Currency		Local/Functional Currency		Group/Reporting Currency	
	Amount	Currency	Amount	Currency	Amount	Currency
1/31 valuated bal.	50,000.00	GBP		EUR	92,006.92	USD
1/31-reval 30/CTA	50,000.00	GBP		EUR	–4,048.13	USD

Exhibit 4.4 Excel Calculation

51

CUMULATIVE REVALUATION "TYPE 10": PERIOD 2 SETUP AND EXECUTION 2/28/2005

In this section, the foreign currency account balances will be revaluated from Transactional Currency (GBP) to Local Currency (EUR). The difference that results from the exchange rate fluctuations on the date of revaluation will be posted in SAP.

Header Data

© SAP AG, 2006

SAP Execution: Execution

Key date 02/28/05
Valuation in Company code currency (10)
Method MEND Month End Valuation Method

G/L acct	Amount in FC	Curr.	Amt in loc.curr.	Amount valuated	Exch.rate	Exch.rate	Ty	Pstg date	Old difference	New difference
140000	50,000.00	GBP	70,525.00	72,610.00	1.45220	1.41050	KR	01/05/2005	0.00	2,085.00
* 140000		GBP	70,525.00						0.00	2,085.00
** 140000			70,525.00						0.00	2,085.00
*** Target Comp. Code UK01			70,525.00						0.00	2,085.00

- **Amount in FC.** This is the document currency (50,000 GBP in this example).

- **Amount in Local Currency.** This is the open item cumulative balance in Local Currency (70,525 EUR in this example).

- **Amount Valuated.** This is the Transaction Currency (50,000 GBP) translated into Local Currency (72,610 EUR) on the key date.

- **Old Difference.** This is the cumulative valuation adjustment that resulted from the prior valuation.

- **New Difference.** This is the current cumulative valuation adjustment, which is the valuated amount, translated into EUR on the key date (72,610 EUR), less the Local Currency amount in EUR (70,525 EUR).

SAP Execution: Posting

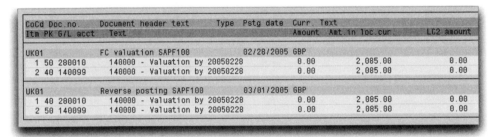

© SAP AG, 2006

- **Amount in Local Currency.** This is the difference between the new valuated amount (72,610 EUR) and the original valuated amount (70,525 EUR).

- **Local Currency 2 Amount.** This is the Local Currency (EUR) revaluated difference translated into Group Currency (USD).

- **Process Batch Session.** If a batch session was created, run transaction SM35 to process the batch session. Select "Process errors only," and Execute.

SAP Execution: Validation

In order to validate the results, select a few G/L accounts to analyze. Use the following steps to compare the revaluation from Transaction to Local Currency:

Step 1. Run SAP transaction code FBL3N for the open items on the key date for the same G/L accounts selected, or select a few to review. Exclude the amounts (Transaction Currency) where they are zero so you do not pick up adjustment amounts. Take the Transaction Currency and convert it to the Local Currency using the exchange rate for the key date being used.

Step 2. Take the original Local Currency (prior period) and the Local Currency amount calculated by the previous step and compare the SAP calculation, Exhibit 4.5.

No Valuation Areas Cumulative Postings	Transaction/ Document Currency		Local/ Functional Currency		Group/ Reporting Currency			Exchange Rates	
	Amount	Currency	Amount	Currency	Amount	Currency		GBP/EUR	EUR/USD
5-Jan	50,000.00	GBP	70,525.00	EUR	96,055.05	USD	M-Rate	1.4105	1.36200
31-Jan	50,000.00	GBP	72,105.00	EUR	94,068.18	USD	Spot-Rate	1.4421	1.30460
28-Feb	50,000.00	GBP	72,610.00	EUR	96,193.73	USD	Spot-Rate	1.4522	1.32480

Period 2	Transaction/ Document Currency		Local/ Functional Currency		Group/ Reporting Currency	
	Amount	Currency	Amount	Currency	Amount	Currency
2/28-reval 10	50,000.00	GBP	2,085.00	EUR		

Exhibit 4.5 Excel Calculation

56

CUMULATIVE REVALUATION "TYPE 30": PERIOD 2 SETUP AND EXECUTION 2/28/2005

In this section, the foreign currency account balances will be revaluated by taking the difference of the EUR/USD exchange rate for the current period and the original period, times the original Local Currency posting. The difference that results from the exchange rate fluctuations on the date of revaluation will be posted in SAP.

Header Information

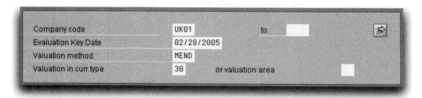

© SAP AG, 2006

CUMULATIVE REVALUATION "TYPE 30": PERIOD 2 EXECUTION 2/28/2005

In this section, the foreign currency account balances will be revaluated by converting the original posting value in Local Currency (EUR) with the difference in exchange rates from period 2 and period 1 for EUR/USD. The difference that results from the exchange rate fluctuations on the date of revaluation will be posted in SAP.

SAP Execution: Execution

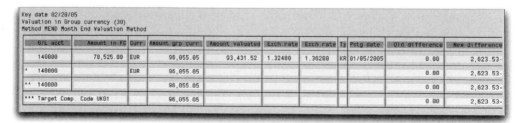

Key date 02/28/05
Valuation in Group currency (30)
Method MEND Month End Valuation Method

G/L acct	Amount in FC	Curr	Amount grp curr	Amount valuated	Exch.rate	Exch.rate	Ty	Pstg date	Old difference	New difference
140000	70,525.00	EUR	96,055.05	93,431.52	1.32480	1.36200	KR	01/05/2005	0.00	2,623.53-
* 140000		EUR	96,055.05						0.00	2,623.53-
** 140000			96,055.05						0.00	2,623.53-
*** Target Comp. Code UK01			96,055.05						0.00	2,623.53-

© SAP AG, 2006

- **Amount in FC.** For group valuation, this is the Local Currency amount in EUR (open item cumulative balance) from the valuation "Type 10" calculation (70,525 EUR in this example).

- **Amount in Group Currency.** This is the open item cumulative balance in Group Currency ($96,055.05 USD in this example).

- **Amount Valuated.** This is the Group Currency on the key date ($96,193.73 USD), less the Local Currency valuation (2,085 EUR), translated into Group Currency $2,762.21 (USD) on key date ($93,431.52 USD in this example).

- **Old Difference.** This is the cumulative valuation adjustment that resulted from the most recent valuation.

- **New Difference.** This is the current cumulative valuation adjustment, which is the valuated amount ($93,431.52 USD) less the original Group Currency amount ($96,055.05 USD).

SAP Execution: Postings

```
CoCd Doc.no.    Document header text    Type  Pstg date  Curr. Text
Itm PK G/L acct   Text                            Amount  Amt.in loc.cur.    LC2 amount

UK01            FC valuation SAPF100         02/28/2005 GBP
   1 40 230010    140000 - Valuation by 20050228      0.00       0.00       2,623.53
   2 50 140099    140000 - Valuation by 20050228      0.00       0.00       2,623.53

UK01            Reverse posting SAPF100      03/01/2005 GBP
   1 50 230010    140000 - Valuation by 20050228      0.00       0.00       2,623.53
   2 40 140099    140000 - Valuation by 20050228      0.00       0.00       2,623.53
```

© SAP AG, 2006

- **Local Currency Amount.** This is not relevant in this valuation method "Type 30."

- **Local Currency 2 Amount.** This is the current amount valuated ($93,431.52 USD) less the original Group Currency amount ($96,055.05 USD).

- **Process Batch Session.** If a batch session was created, run transaction SM35 to process the batch session. Select "Process errors only," and Execute.

SAP Execution: Validation

No Valuation Areas Cumulative Postings	Transaction/ Document Currency		Local/ Functional Currency		Group/ Reporting Currency			Exchange Rates	
	Amount	Currency	Amount	Currency	Amount	Currency		GBP/EUR	EUR/USD
5-Jan	50,000.00	GBP	70,525.00	EUR	96,055.05	USD	M-Rate	1.4105	1.36200
31-Jan	50,000.00	GBP	72,105.00	EUR	94,068.18	USD	Spot-Rate	1.4421	1.30460
28-Feb	50,000.00	GBP	72,610.00	EUR	96,193.73	USD	Spot-Rate	1.4522	1.32480

Period 2	Transaction/ Document Currency		Local/ Functional Currency		Group/ Reporting Currency	
	Amount	Currency	Amount	Currency	Amount	Currency
2/28- valuated bal.	50,000.00	GBP		EUR	93,431.52	USD
2/28-reval 30/CTA	50,000.00	GBP		EUR	−2,623.53	USD

INCREMENTAL REVALUATION "TYPE 10": PERIOD 1 SETUP AND EXECUTION 1/31/2005

In this section, the foreign currency account balances will be revaluated by converting the Transaction Currency posting (GBP) to Local Currency (EUR) using the exchange rate for the original posting, and the Transaction Currency posting (GBP) to Local Currency (EUR) using the exchange rate for the evaluation key date. The difference that results from the exchange rate fluctuations on the date of revaluation will be posted in SAP.

Header Data

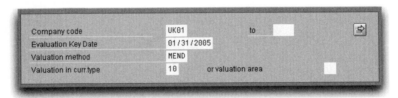

© SAP AG, 2006

Postings Tab

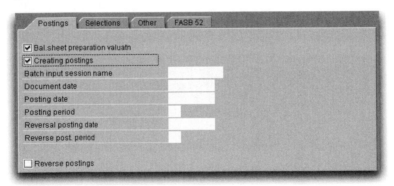

© SAP AG, 2006

SAP Execution: Execution

Key date 01/31/05
Valuation in Company code currency (10)
Method MEND Month End Valuation Method

G/L acct	Amount in FC	Curr.	Amt. in loc.cur.	Amount valuated	Exch.rate	Exch.rate	Ty	Pstg date	Old difference	New difference
140000	50,000.00	GBP	70,525.00	72,105.00	1.44210	1.41050	KR	01/05/2005	0.00	1,580.00
* 140000		GBP	70,525.00						0.00	1,580.00
** 140000			70,525.00						0.00	1,580.00
*** Target Comp. Code UK01			70,525.00						0.00	1,580.00

- **Amount in FC.** This is the document currency (50,000 GBP in this example).

- **Amount in Local Currency.** This is the open item cumulative balance in Local Currency (70,525 EUR in this example).

- **Amount Valuated.** This is the Transaction Currency (50,000 GBP) translated into Local Currency (72,105 EUR) on the key date.

- **Old Difference.** This is the cumulative valuation adjustment that resulted from the prior valuation.

- **New Difference.** This is the current cumulative valuation adjustment, which is the valuated amount, Transaction Currency translated into EUR on the key date (72,105 EUR), less the original Local Currency amount in EUR (70,525 EUR).

SAP Execution: Posting

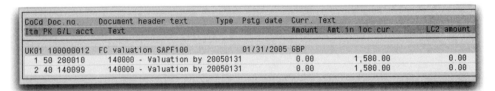

- **Amount in Local Currency.** This is the difference between the new valuated amount (72,105 EUR) and the previous valuated amount (70,525 EUR).

- **Local Currency 2 Amount.** This is the Local Currency (EUR) revaluated difference translated into Group Currency (USD). This is not executed or posted with this process method.

- **Process Batch Session.** If a batch session was created, run transaction SM35 to process the batch session. Select "Process errors only," and Execute.

SAP Execution: Validation

No Valuation Areas Incremental Postings	Transaction/ Document Currency		Local/ Functional Currency		Group/ Reporting Currency				Exchange Rates	
	Amount	Currency	Amount	Currency	Amount	Currency			GBP/EUR	EUR/USD
5-Jan	50,000.00	GBP	70,525.00	EUR	96,055.05	USD	M-Rate		1.4105	1.36200
31-Jan	50,000.00	GBP	72,105.00	EUR	94,068.18	USD	Spot-Rate		1.4421	1.30460
28-Feb	50,000.00	GBP	72,610.00	EUR	96,193.73	USD	Spot-Rate		1.4522	1.32480

Period 1	Transaction/ Document Currency		Local/ Functional Currency		Group/ Reporting Currency	
	Amount	Currency	Amount	Currency	Amount	Currency
1/31-reval 10	50,000.00	GBP	1,580.00	EUR		

INCREMENTAL REVALUATION "TYPE 30": PERIOD 1 SETUP AND EXECUTION 1/31/2005

In this section, the foreign currency account balances will be revaluated by converting the Local Currency posting (EUR) to Local Currency 2/Group Currency (USD) using the exchange rate for the original posting, and the Local Currency posting (EUR) to Local Currency 2/Group Currency (USD) using the exchange rate for period 1. The difference that results from the exchange rate fluctuations on the date of revaluation will be posted in SAP.

Header Information

© SAP AG, 2006

Postings Tab

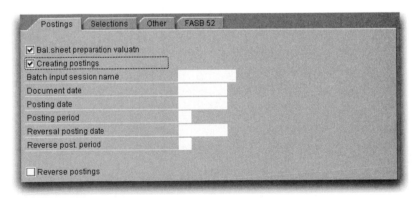

© SAP AG, 2006

SAP Execution: Execution

Key date 01/31/05
Valuation in Group currency (30)
Method MEND Month End Valuation Method

G/L acct	Amount in FC	Curr.	Amount grp curr.	Amount valuated	Exch.rate	Exch.rate	Ty	Pstg date	Old difference	New difference
140000	72,105.00	EUR	96,055.05	94,068.18	1.30460	1.33216	KR	01/05/2005	0.00	1,986.87-
* 140000		EUR	96,055.05						0.00	1,986.87-
** 140000			96,055.05						0.00	1,986.87-
*** Target Comp. Code UK01			96,055.05						0.00	1,986.87-

65

- **Amount in FC.** For group valuation, this is the Local Currency amount in EUR (open item cumulative balance) from the valuation "Type 10" calculation (72,105 EUR in this example).

- **Amount in Group Currency.** This is the open item cumulative balance in Group Currency ($96,055.05 USD in this example).

- **Amount Valuated.** This is the Group Currency on the key date ($94,068.18 USD).

- **Old Difference.** This is the cumulative valuation adjustment that resulted from the most recent valuation.

- **New Difference.** This is the amount valuated ($94,068.18 USD) less the amount in Group Currency ($96,055.05 USD), $1,986.87 USD in this example.

SAP Execution: Posting

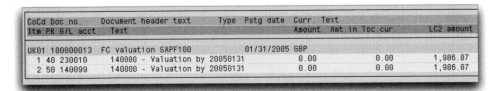

© SAP AG, 2006

- **Local Currency Amount.** This is not relevant in this valuation method "Type 30."

- **Local Currency 2 Amount.** This is the current amount valuated ($94,068.18 USD) less the prior period Group Currency amount ($96,055.05 USD).

- **Process Batch Session.** If a batch session was created, run transaction SM35 to process the batch session. Select "Process errors only," and Execute.

SAP Execution: Validation

No Valuation Areas Incremental Postings	Transaction/ Document Currency		Local/ Functional Currency		Group/ Reporting Currency			Exchange Rates	
	Amount	Currency	Amount	Currency	Amount	Currency		GBP/EUR	EUR/USD
5-Jan	50,000.00	GBP	70,525.00	EUR	96,055.05	USD	M-Rate	1.4105	1.36200
31-Jan	50,000.00	GBP	72,105.00	EUR	94,068.18	USD	Spot-Rate	1.4421	1.30460
28-Feb	50,000.00	GBP	72,610.00	EUR	96,193.73	USD	Spot-Rate	1.4522	1.32480

Period 1	Transaction/ Document Currency		Local/ Functional Currency		Group/ Reporting Currency	
	Amount	Currency	Amount	Currency	Amount	Currency
1/31-reval 30	50,000.00	GBP		EUR	−1,986.87	

INCREMENTAL REVALUATION "TYPE 10": PERIOD 2 SETUP AND EXECUTION 2/28/2005

In this section, the foreign currency account balances will be revaluated by converting the Transaction Currency posting (GBP) to Local Currency (EUR) using the exchange rate for period 1, and the Transaction Currency posting (GBP) to Local Currency (EUR) using the exchange rate for period 2. The difference that results from the exchange rate fluctuations on the date of revaluation will be posted in SAP.

Header Data

© SAP AG, 2006

Postings Tab

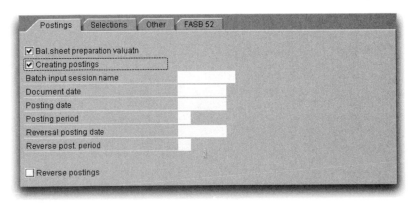

© SAP AG, 2006

SAP Execution: Execution

Key date 02/28/05
Valuation in Company code currency (10)
Method MEND Month End Valuation Method

G/L acct	Amount in FC	Curr.	Amt in loc.cur	Amount valuated	Exch.rate	Exch.rate	Ty	Pstg date	Old difference	New difference
140000	50,000.00	GBP	70,525.00	72,610.00	1.45220	1.41050	KR	01/05/2005	1,580.00	2,085.00
* 140000		GBP	70,525.00						1,580.00	2,085.00
** 140000			70,525.00						1,580.00	2,085.00
*** Target Comp. Code UK01			70,525.00						1,580.00	2,085.00

© SAP AG, 2006

69

- **Amount in FC.** This is the document currency (50,000 GBP in this example).

- **Amount in Local Currency.** This is the open item cumulative balance in Local Currency (70,525 EUR in this example).

- **Amount Valuated.** This is the Transaction Currency (50,000 GBP) translated into Local Currency (72,610 EUR) on the key date.

- **Old Difference.** This is the cumulative valuation adjustment that resulted from the prior valuation.

- **New Difference.** This is the current cumulative valuation adjustment, which is the valuated amount, Transaction Currency translated into EUR on the key date (72,610 EUR), less the previous Local Currency amount in EUR (72,105 EUR).

SAP Execution: Posting

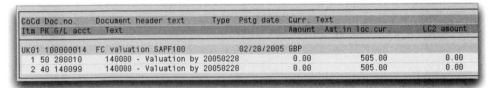

© SAP AG, 2006

- **Amount in Local Currency.** This is the difference between the new valuated amount (72,610 EUR) and the previous valuated amount (72,105 EUR).

- **Local Currency 2 Amount.** This is the Local Currency (EUR) revaluated difference translated into Group Currency (USD). This is not executed or posted with this process method.

- **Process Batch Session.** If a batch session was created, run transaction SM35 to process the batch session. Select "Process errors only," and Execute.

SAP Execution: Validation

No Valuation Areas Incremental Postings	Transaction/ Document Currency		Local/ Functional Currency		Group/ Reporting Currency			Exchange Rates	
	Amount	Currency	Amount	Currency	Amount	Currency		GBP/EUR	EUR/USD
5-Jan	50,000.00	GBP	70,525.00	EUR	96,055.05	USD	M-Rate	1.4105	1.36200
31-Jan	50,000.00	GBP	72,105.00	EUR	94,068.18	USD	Spot-Rate	1.4421	1.30460
28-Feb	50,000.00	GBP	72,610.00	EUR	96,193.73	USD	Spot-Rate	1.4522	1.32480

Period 2	Transaction/ Document Currency		Local/ Functional Currency		Group/ Reporting Currency	
	Amount	Currency	Amount	Currency	Amount	Currency
2/28-reval 10	50,000.00	GBP	505.00	EUR		

INCREMENTAL REVALUATION "TYPE 30": PERIOD 2 SETUP AND EXECUTION 2/28/2005

In this section, the foreign currency account balances will be revaluated by converting the Local Currency posting (EUR) to Local Currency 2/Group Currency (USD) using the exchange rate for period 1, and the Local Currency posting (EUR) to Local Currency 2/Group Currency (USD) using the exchange rate for period 2. The difference that results from the exchange rate fluctuations on the date of revaluation will be posted in SAP.

Header Information

© SAP AG, 2006

Postings Tab

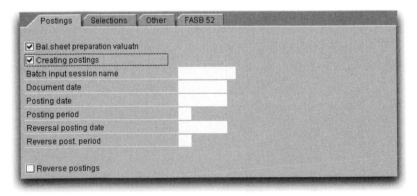

© SAP AG, 2006

SAP Execution: Execution

Key date 02/28/05
Valuation in Group currency (30)
Method MEND Month End Valuation Method

G/L acct	Amount in FC	Curr	Amount grp curr	Amount valuated	Exch.rate	Exch.rate	Ty	Pstg date	Old difference	New difference
140000	72,610.00	EUR	96,055.05	96,193.73	1.32480	1.32289	KR	01/05/2005	1,986.87-	138.68
* 140000		EUR	96,055.05						1,986.87-	138.68
** 140000			96,055.05						1,986.87-	138.68
*** Target Comp. Code UK01			96,055.05						1,986.87-	138.68

© SAP AG, 2006

73

- **Amount in FC.** For group valuation, this is the Local Currency amount in EUR (open item cumulative balance) from the valuation "Type 10" calculation (72,610 EUR in this example).

- **Amount in Group Currency.** This is the open item cumulative balance in Group Currency ($96,055.05 USD in this example).

- **Amount Valuated.** This is the Group Currency on the key date ($96,193.73 USD).

- **Old Difference.** This is the cumulative valuation adjustment that resulted from the most recent valuation (–$1,986.87 USD in this example).

- **New Difference.** This is the amount valuated ($96,193.73 USD) less the amount in Group Currency ($96,055.05 USD); $138.68 USD in this example.

SAP Execution: Posting

CoCd Doc.no.	Document header text	Type	Pstg date	Curr.	Text		
Itm PK G/L acct	Text				Amount	Amt.in loc.cur.	LC2 amount
UK01 100000015	FC valuation SAPF100		02/28/2005	GBP			
1 50 280010	140000 - Valuation by 20050228				0.00	0.00	2,125.55
2 40 140099	140000 - Valuation by 20050228				0.00	0.00	2,125.55

© SAP AG, 2006

- **Local Currency Amount.** This is not relevant in this valuation method "Type 30."

- **Local Currency 2 Amount.** This is the current amount valuated ($96,193.73 USD) less the prior period Group Currency amount ($94,068.18 USD).

- **Process Batch Session.** If a batch session was created, run transaction SM35 to process the batch session. Select "Process errors only," and Execute.

SAP Execution: Validation

No Valuation Areas Incremental Postings	Transaction/ Document Currency		Local/ Functional Currency		Group/ Reporting Currency			Exchange Rates	
	Amount	Currency	Amount	Currency	Amount	Currency		GBP/EUR	EUR/USD
5-Jan	50,000.00	GBP	70,525.00	EUR	96,055.05	USD	M-Rate	1.4105	1.36200
31-Jan	50,000.00	GBP	72,105.00	EUR	94,068.18	USD	Spot-Rate	1.4421	1.30460
28-Feb	50,000.00	GBP	72,610.00	EUR	96,193.73	USD	Spot-Rate	1.4522	1.32480

Period 2	Transaction/ Document Currency		Local/ Functional Currency		Group/ Reporting Currency	
	Amount	Currency	Amount	Currency	Amount	Currency
2/28-reval 30	50,000.00	GBP		EUR	2,125.55	

5

REVALUATION WITH FULL VALUATION AREAS

HIGHLIGHTS

- Revaluation "Type 10": Period 1 Setup and Execution
- Revaluation "Type 30": Period 1 Setup and Execution
- Revaluation "Type 10": Period 2 Setup and Execution
- Revaluation "Type 30": Period 2 Setup and Execution
- Unique Configuration

This method of revaluation revaluates the G/L accounts using only valuation areas. The end result is a revaluated balance from Transaction Currency to Local Currency with the Gain/Loss posting as well as with translation and associated CTA posting. Refer to SAP Note No. 448306 in the References at the end of the book.

Additionally, postings are done in *full* each time revaluation is run. Reversals are done in *full* before each revaluation run. Incremental postings are not possible with this method of execution.

This method does provide for translation, but it also requires that revaluation runs are executed in full, and reversed in full before each execution (no incremental postings), which can lead to long run times. SAP address this in SAP Note No. 692693 (see the References).

The calculations for this methodology are similar to method 3 (revaluation with one valuation area), but the benefits for method 3 are that only one valuation area is required, and the additional account assignment table does not

	Transaction is Accessed via:
Via Menus	Accounting → Financial Accounting → General Ledger → Periodic Processing → Closing → Valuate → Foreign Currency Valuation (Exhibit 5.2)
Via Transaction Code	F.05

Exhibit 5.1   Access Sequence

have to be maintained. The original account assignment table (V-T030H) can still be used.

It is also much more difficult to configure the table required for support of the valuation area account assignments (T030HB). Additionally, SAP currently has no indicator that lets you know you have already run the revaluation for a period using valuation areas. Therefore, revaluation can be mistakenly run multiple times. This method of execution is not commonly run.

SAP provides a means to execute foreign currency revaluation on specific G/L accounts managed in foreign currencies. Exhibit 5.1 describes the menu path and transaction code, and Exhibit 5.2 shows it on the menu. Transaction code F.05 allows the revaluation of one or more accounts at the same time. The following steps occur with currency revaluation execution:

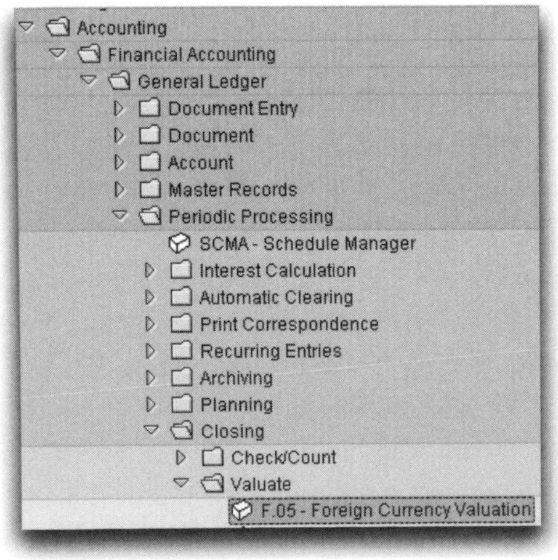

Exhibit 5.2   Menu Path

© SAP AG, 2006

1. Each G/L account's line item selected is revalued using the exchange rate of the key evaluation date.

2. A posting is generated to the appropriate unrealized Gain/Loss account and balance statement adjustment account.

3. A reversal posting is generated in total for the next day (unless you specify another date to reverse the postings to the unrealized Gain/ Loss).

Currency revaluation has various configurations that are required:

- Exchange rate types are set up.
- Valuation methods are set up (OB59).
- Document types are set up (OBA7).
- Exchange rates are entered for each currency (OC41).
- Account determination has been defined (OBA1).
- Posting keys are assigned for adjustment postings.

REVALUATION "TYPE 10": PERIOD 1 SETUP AND EXECUTION 1/31/2005

In this section, the foreign currency account balances will be revaluated by converting the Transaction Currency posting (GBP) to Local Currency (EUR) using the exchange rate for the original posting, and the Transaction Currency posting (GBP) to Local Currency (EUR) using the exchange rate for the evaluation key date. The difference that results from the exchange rate fluctuations on the date of revaluation will be posted in SAP.

Header Data

- **Company Code.** Select the company code or company codes that are to be revaluated. Some companies prefer to centralize this function, whereas other companies decentralize it. Either way, you can run it for one or more company codes at the same time. It depends on how you want to analyze the output.

> When you run this for multiple company codes, the G/L accounts that are selected for revaluation are run for all companies selected. For example, a specific G/L account (e.g., 2050) might exist in all company codes, but revaluation runs might only be desired in one or a select number of company codes. If company codes have different G/Ls that require revaluation, it might be best to run the company codes separately.

- **Evaluation Key Date.** The evaluation key date is used to determine the date of the currency exchange rates used in the revaluation. SAP will look for the exchange rate that falls on the key date entered. If one does not exist for that specific date, it will look for the exchange rate for the closest date prior to the date entered as the evaluation key date. The evaluation key date should be the last day of the period.

    The evaluation key date is also used to evaluate open item documents that have not been cleared as of this date (periods 13 to 16 are considered if the key date is within period 12).

- **Valuation Method.** Valuation method is the key that determines a foreign currency valuation method/approach used when carrying out the foreign currency revaluation. The most important field read from the valuation method is the type of exchange rate used (average or spot). Refer to the common configuration area to read more information specific to this key.

- **Valuation in Currency Type or Valuation Area.** Valuation currency type defines the type of valuation being performed. First Local Currency type for valuation defines the currency type for Transactional Currency to Local Currency valuation ("type 10" in these examples).

Postings Tab

© SAP AG, 2006

- **Balance Sheet Preparation Valuation.** This parameter can only be used for valuation runs that do not use valuation areas. This indicator does not have an effect on non–open item accounts; it only affects open item accounts.

  For open item accounts, this indicator is key. If *not* selected, reversals will be posted and valuation will be cumulative. If selected, no reversal postings will occur and valuation will be incremental. Refer to SAP Note No. 87538 in the References. Most companies that run revaluation via this method (e.g., not using valuation areas) do not reverse postings and post incrementally.

  To post reversals for non–open item accounts, select the "reverse postings" indicator at the bottom under "For G/L Account Balance Valuation" and choose a date. To post reversals for both open item and non–open item accounts, do not select the "balance sheet preparation valuation indicator" and select the "reverse postings" indicator at the bottom.

- **Create Postings.** Leave this indicator blank to run the valuation in test mode. Select the indicator to make the postings in FI. When selected, the postings can either be executed immediately in the foreground, in the background, or a batch input session can be specified.

- **Batch Input Session Name.** If you enter a name here, a batch input session with that name will be created. Transaction SM35 must be used to process the batch session. The postings will not be made until the batch session is processed. If you do not enter a name here, the postings will be made immediately.

- **Document Date.** The document date of the unrealized postings can be specified here or SAP will default to the valuation key date.

- **Posting Date.** The posting date of the unrealized postings can be specified here or SAP will default to the valuation key date.

- **Posting Period.** Posting period in which the valuation postings are generated. The number entered should correspond to the period that includes the posting date or valuation key date.

- **Reversal Posting Date.** The posting date of the reversal postings can be specified here; otherwise, SAP will default to the next day. This is normally the first day of the next period or the next day if running valuation daily. This is for non–open item accounts only.

- **Reversal Posting Period.** This is the posting period in which the valuation postings are generated. This must correspond to the posting date. This is for non–open item accounts only.

- **Reverse Postings.** This indicator affects the valuation of non–open items only. If not selected, the G/L balances for non–open item accounts will not be reversed. If selected, they will be reversed in full.

Selections Tab

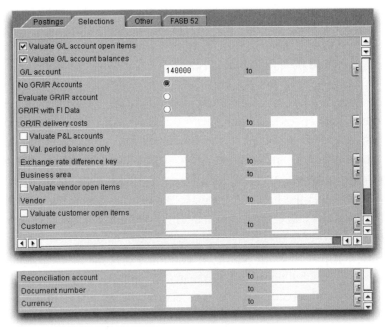

© SAP AG, 2006

- **Valuate G/L Account Open Items.** Select this indicator in combination with identifying the specific open item G/L accounts to be valuated.

- **Valuate G/L Account Balances.** Select this indicator in combination with identifying the specific G/L balance accounts to be valuated.

- **G/L Account.** Identify the specific open item G/L account(s) that will be revaluated. These same G/L accounts will appear in the G/L balance tab, and even if the "Valuate G/L Account Open Items" indicator is selected, the accounts identified in both the open items and G/L balance tab will be valuated based on their G/L account definition as open item or line item. If a range of G/L accounts that include both open item and non–open item accounts is identified, and only the "Valuate G/L Account Open Items" indicator is selected, then only the G/L accounts in the range that are open item will be revaluated.

- **No GR/IR Accounts.** If selected, no GR/IR valuation will occur. GR/IR should be revaluated.

- **Evaluate GR/IR Accounts.** If selected, open items with a goods receipt (MIGO) will be valuated in the GR/IR account. The Purchase Order Currency is then valuated. The valuation is only completed if the goods receipt has occurred, because this is when the first financial posting occurs. The GR/IR account is an open item account, and postings will automatically be reversed. Revaluation occurs based on the Purchase Order Currency. Refer to SAP Note No. 441333 in the References for more information.

- **GR/IR with FI Data.** If you select this indicator, revaluation will occur on *all* items in the GR/IR account. U.S. clients may choose to use this field as opposed to the previous field because this gives more control to the person running the revaluation.

- **GR/IR Delivery Costs.** Specify accounts for GR/IR transaction cost postings. Transactions with debit balances (invoices without goods) should not be valuated. The vendor invoice will be valuated. Goods delivered but not invoiced will be valuated with this indicator setting.

- **Valuate P&L Accounts.** Select to valuate P&L accounts. This is not normally selected unless fixed asset depreciation is being revaluated. Do not reverse P&L postings.

- **Valuate Period Balance Only.** This is not normally selected unless running revaluation on P&L accounts. Selecting this indicator valuates the period balance and not the cumulative balance.

- **Exchange Rate Difference Key.** If exchange rate difference keys are utilized on G/L account master data for non–open item accounts, this field can be used to uniquely identify the valuation for specific exchange rate keys.

- **Business Area.** Revaluation can be run for specific business areas (if business areas are used).

- **Valuate Vendor Open Items.** To valuate vendor (payables) open items, select this indicator and select the appropriate vendors or range of vendors in the next field.

- **Vendor.** Select the vendor(s) or range of vendors to valuate along with the previous indicator "Value Vendor Open Items."

- **Valuate Customer Open Items.** To valuate customer (receivable) open items, select this indicator and select the appropriate customers or range of customers in the next field.

- **Customer.** Select the customer(s) or range of customers to valuate, along with the previous indicator "Valuate Customer Open Items."

- **Reconciliation Account.** This field can be used as an alternative to listing the vendors or customers. The vendor or customer reconciliation accounts are listed here. If used, only vendors (or customers) assigned to this G/L reconciliation account(s) will be valuated.

- **Document Number.** This is used to select one or more specific documents for valuation. This is not normally used for production runs but is useful in testing valuation so that valuation and postings are kept to a specific document test.

- **Currency.** Valuation runs can be limited to execution by currency. To run revaluation on just GBP currency, enter this information. Leaving this field blank will select all open items for valuation for any currency.

- **SL Extra.** Split ledger functionality in SAP R/3 v4.7 allows you to distribute valuation differences to profit centers or business areas based on how the split ledger ZZPLIT is set up.

REVALUATION WITH FULL VALUATION AREAS

Other Tab

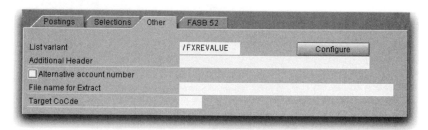

© SAP AG, 2006

- **List Variant.** The list variant is useful in displaying all of the balances SAP uses to calculate the valuation postings.

- **Additional Header.** A report header/description can be entered here, and it will be entered on the valuation report.

- **Alternative Account Number.** If selected, the alternative account number defined on the G/L account master record is used. This is normally used if a country chart of accounts is maintained in the company codes selected. Remember that the financial statements will need to be updated to include the alternative accounts. Normally, this is not selected.

- **File Name for Extract.** Enter a file name if an extract is desired. Otherwise, leave this field blank.

- **Target Co-code.** A cross-company code can be entered for the valuation postings. Normally, this is left blank.

FASB 52 Tab

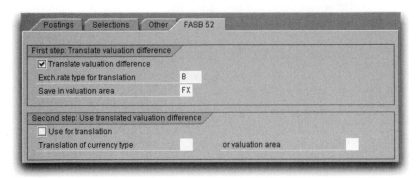

In this first step, foreign currency Transaction Currency items are valuated and posted to P&L accounts in the Local Currency. Additionally, the valuation difference is translated into Group Currency and posted. The difference that is translated into Group Currency is stored in the valuation area FX.

- **Translate Valuation Difference.** Select this indicator to execute the translation using valuation areas.
- **Exchange Rate Type for Translation.** Select the appropriate exchange rate type.
- **Save in Valuation Area.** Select this indicator to store the valuation in valuation area FX.
- **Use for Translation.** This is not used for revaluation "type 10" (Transaction to Local Currency). This is used for the second step, revaluation 30 (Transaction to Group Currency).
- **Translation of Currency Type or Valuation Area.** This is not used for revaluation "type 10" (Transaction to Local Currency). This is used for the second step, revaluation 30 (Transaction to Group Currency).

SAP Execution: Execution

Key date 01/31/05
Valuation in Company code currency (10)
Method MEND Month End Valuation Method

G/L acct	Amount in FC	Curr.	Amt.in loc.cur.	Amount valuated	Exch.rate	Exch.rate	Ty	Pstg date	Old difference	New difference
140000	50,000.00	GBP	70,525.00	72,105.00	1.44210	1.41050	KR	01/05/2005	0.00	1,580.00
* 140000		GBP	70,525.00						0.00	1,580.00
** 140000			70,525.00						0.00	1,580.00
*** Target Comp. Code UK01			70,525.00						0.00	1,580.00

- **Amount in FC.** This is the document currency (50,000 GBP in this example).

- **Amount in Local Currency.** This is the open item cumulative balance in Local Currency (70,525 EUR in this example).

- **Amount Valuated.** This is the Transaction Currency (50,000 GBP) translated into Local Currency (72,105 EUR in this example) on the key date.

- **Old Difference.** This is the cumulative valuation adjustment that resulted from the prior valuation.

- **New Difference.** This is the current cumulative valuation adjustment, which is the valuated amount, Transaction Currency translated into EUR on the key date (72,105 EUR), less the Local Currency amount in EUR (70,525 EUR).

SAP Execution: Posting

CoCd Doc.no.	Document header text	Type	Pstg date	Curr. Text		
Itm PK G/L acct	Text			Amount	Amt.in loc.cur.	LC2 amount
UK01	FC valuation SAPF100		01/31/2005	GBP		
1 50 280010	140000 - Valuation by 20050131			0.00	1,580.00	2,061.27
2 40 140099	140000 - Valuation by 20050131			0.00	1,580.00	2,061.27
UK01	Reverse posting SAPF100		02/01/2005	GBP		
1 40 280010	140000 - Valuation by 20050131			0.00	1,580.00	2,061.27
2 50 140099	140000 - Valuation by 20050131			0.00	1,580.00	2,061.27

© SAP AG, 2006

- **Amount in Local Currency.** This is the difference between the old valuated amount and the new valuated amount.

- **Local Currency 2 Amount.** This is the Local Currency (1,580 EUR) revaluated difference translated into Group Currency ($2,061.27 USD).

- **Process Batch Session.** If a batch session was created, run transaction SM35 to process the batch session. Select "Process errors only," and Execute.

SAP Execution: Validation

In order to validate the results, select a few G/L accounts to analyze. Use the following steps to compare the revaluation from Transaction to Local Currency:

Step 1. Run FBL3N for the open items on the key date for the same G/L accounts selected, or select a few to review. Exclude the amounts (Transaction Currency) where they are zero so you do not pick up adjustment amounts. Take the Transaction Currency and convert it to the Local Currency using the exchange rate for the key date being used.

Step 2. Take the original Local Currency (prior period) and the Local Currency amount calculated by the previous step and compare the SAP calculation, Exhibit 5.3.

Multiple Valuation Areas	Transaction/ Document Currency		Local/ Functional Currency		Group/ Reporting Currency			Exchange Rates	
	Amount	Currency	Amount	Currency	Amount	Currency		GBP/EUR	EUR/USD
5-Jan	50,000.00	GBP	70,525.00	EUR	96,055.05	USD	M-Rate	1.4105	1.36200
31-Jan	50,000.00	GBP	72,105.00	EUR	94,068.18	USD	Spot-Rate	1.4421	1.30460
28-Feb	50,000.00	GBP	72,610.00	EUR	96,193.73	USD	Spot-Rate	1.4522	1.32480

Period 1	Transaction/ Document Currency		Local/ Functional Currency		Group/ Reporting Currency	
	Amount	Currency	Amount	Currency	Amount	Currency
1/31-reval 10	50,000.00	GBP	1,580.00	EUR	2,061.27	USD

Exhibit 5.3   Excel Calculation

REVALUATION "TYPE 30": PERIOD 1 SETUP AND EXECUTION 1/31/2005

In this section, the cumulative balance is calculated by taking the revaluated amount from the revaluation "Type 10" calculation, translated into Group Currency, and adding the original Group Currency translated balance. The difference between this amount and Group Currency translated on the key date is the cumulative translation adjustment posted in SAP.

Header Data

- **Company Code.** Select the company code or company codes that are to be revaluated. Some companies prefer to centralize this function, whereas other companies decentralize it. Either way, you can run it for one or more company codes at the same time. It depends on how you want to analyze the output.

> When you run this for multiple company codes, the G/L accounts that are selected for revaluation are run for all companies selected. For example, a specific G/L account (e.g., 2050) might exist in all company codes, but revaluation runs might only be desired in one or a select number of company codes. If company codes have different G/Ls that require revaluation, it might be best to run the company codes individually.

- **Evaluation Key Date.** The evaluation key date is used to determine the date of the currency exchange rates used in the revaluation. SAP will look for the exchange rate that falls on the key date entered. If one does

91

not exist for that specific date, it will look for the exchange rate for the closest date prior to the date entered as the evaluation key date. The evaluation key date should be the last day of the period.

The evaluation key date is also used to evaluate open item documents that have not been cleared as of this date (periods 13 through 16 are considered if the key date is within period 12).

- **Valuation Method.** Valuation method is the key that determines a foreign currency valuation method/approach used when carrying out the foreign currency revaluation. The most important field read from the valuation method is the type of exchange rate used (average or spot). Refer to the common configuration area to read more information that is specific to this key.

- **Valuation in Currency Type or Valuation Area.** Valuation currency type defines the type of valuation being performed. Second Local Currency type is defined for Local Currency to Global Currency valuation ("Type 30" in these examples).

Postings Tab

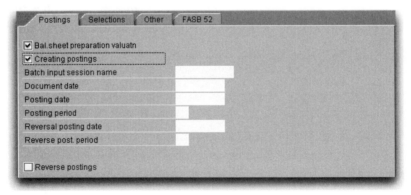

© SAP AG, 2006

- **Balance Sheet Preparation Valuation.** This parameter can only be used for valuation runs that do not use valuation areas. This indicator does not have an effect on non–open item accounts; it only affects open item accounts.

For open item accounts, this indicator is key. If *not* selected, reversals will be posted and valuation will be cumulative. If selected, no reversal postings will occur and valuation will be incremental. Refer to SAP Note No. 87538 in the References. Most companies that run revaluation via this method (e.g., not using valuation areas) do not reverse postings and post incrementally.

To post reversals for non–open item accounts, select the "reverse postings" indicator at the bottom under "For G/L Account Balance Valuation" and choose a date. To post reversals for both open item and non–open item accounts, do not select the "balance sheet preparation valuation" indicator and select the "reverse postings" indicator at the bottom.

- **Create Postings.** Leave this indicator blank to run the valuation in test mode. Select the indicator to make the postings in FI. When selected, the postings can either be executed immediately in the foreground, in the background, or a batch input session can be specified.

- **Batch Input Session Name.** If you enter a name here, a batch input session with that name will be created. Transaction SM35 must be used to process the batch session. The postings will not be made until the batch session is processed. If you do not enter a name here, the postings will be made immediately.

- **Document Date.** The document date of the unrealized postings can be specified here or SAP will default to the valuation key date.

- **Posting Date.** The posting date of the unrealized postings can be specified here or SAP will default to the valuation key date.

- **Posting Period.** Posting period in which the valuation postings are generated. The number entered should correspond to the period that includes the posting date or valuation key date.

- **Reversal Posting Date.** The posting date of the reversal postings can be specified here; otherwise, SAP will default to the next day. This is normally the first day of the next period or the next day if running valuation daily. This is for non–open item accounts only.

- **Reversal Posting Period.** This is the posting period in which the valuation postings are generated. This must correspond to the posting date. This is for non–open item accounts only.

- **Reverse Postings.** This indicator affects the valuation of non–open items only. If not selected, the G/L balances for non–open item accounts will not be reversed. If selected, they will be reversed in full.

Selections Tab

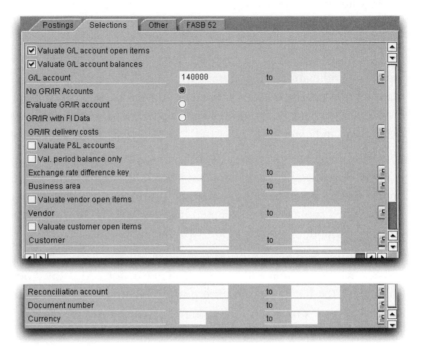

© SAP AG, 2006

- **Valuate G/L Account Open Items.** Select this indicator in combination with identifying the specific open item G/L accounts to be valuated.

- **Valuate G/L Account Balances.** Select this indicator in combination with identifying the specific G/L balance accounts to be valuated.

- **G/L Account.** Identify the specific open item G/L account(s) that will be revaluated. These same G/L accounts will appear in the G/L balance tab, and even if the "Valuate G/L Account Open Items" indicator is selected, the accounts identified in both the open items and G/L balance tab will be valuated based on their G/L account definition as open item or line item. If a range of G/L accounts that include both open item and non–open item accounts is identified, and only the "Valuate G/L Account Open Items" indicator is selected, then only the G/L accounts in the range that are open item will be revaluated.

- **No GR/IR Accounts.** If selected, no GR/IR valuation will occur. GR/IR should be revaluated.

- **Evaluate GR/IR Accounts.** If selected, open items with a goods receipt (MIGO) will be valuated in the GR/IR account. The Purchase Order Currency is then valuated. The valuation is only completed if the goods receipt has occurred, because this is when the first financial posting occurs. The GR/IR account is an open item account, and postings will automatically be reversed. Revaluation occurs based on the Purchase Order Currency. Refer to SAP Note No. 441333 in the References for more information.

- **GR/IR with FI Data.** If you select this indicator, revaluation will occur on *all* items in the GR/IR account. U.S. clients may choose to use this field as opposed to the previous field because this gives more control to the person running the revaluation.

- **GR/IR Delivery Costs.** Specify accounts for GR/IR transaction cost postings. Transactions with debit balances (invoices without goods) should not be valuated. The vendor invoice will be valuated. Goods delivered but not invoiced will be valuated with this indicator setting.

- **Valuate P&L Accounts.** Select to valuate P&L accounts. This is not normally selected unless fixed asset depreciation is being revaluated. Do not reverse P&L postings.

- **Valuate Period Balance Only.** This is not normally selected unless running revaluation on P&L accounts. Selecting this indicator valuates the period balance and not the cumulative balance.

- **Exchange Rate Difference Key.** If exchange rate difference keys are utilized on G/L account master data for non–open item accounts, this field can be used to uniquely identify the valuation for specific exchange rate keys.

- **Business Area.** Revaluation can be run for specific business areas (if business areas are used).

- **Valuate Vendor Open Items.** To valuate vendor (payables) open items, select this indicator and select the appropriate vendors or range of vendors in the next field.

- **Vendor.** Select the vendor(s) or range of vendors to valuate along with the previous indicator "Value Vendor Open Items."

- **Valuate Customer Open Items.** To valuate customer (receivable) open items, select this indicator and select the appropriate customers or range of customers in the next field.

- **Customer.** Select the customer(s) or range of customers to valuate, along with the previous indicator "Valuate Customer Open Items."

- **Reconciliation Account.** This field can be used as an alternative to listing the vendors or customers. The vendor or customer reconciliation accounts are listed here. If used, only vendors (or customers) assigned to this G/L reconciliation account(s) will be valuated.

- **Document Number.** This is used to select one or more specific documents for valuation. This is not normally used for production runs but is useful in testing valuation so that valuation and postings are kept to a specific document test.

- **Currency.** Valuations runs can be limited to execution by currency. To run revaluation on just GBP currency, enter this information. Leaving this field blank will select all open items for valuation for any currency.

- **SL Extra.** Split ledger functionality in SAP R/3 v4.7 allows you to distribute valuation differences to profit centers or business areas based on how the split ledger ZZPLIT is set up.

Other Tab

© SAP AG, 2006

- **List Variant.** The list variant is useful in displaying all of the balances SAP uses to calculate the valuation postings.

- **Additional Header.** A report header/description can be entered here, and it will be entered on the valuation report.

- **Alternative Account Number.** If selected, the alternative account number defined on the G/L account master record is used. This is normally used if a country chart of accounts is maintained in the company codes selected. Remember that the financial statements will need to be updated to include the alternative accounts. Normally, this is not selected.

- **File Name for Extract.** Enter a file name if an extract is desired. Otherwise, leave this field blank.

- **Target Co-code.** A cross-company code can be entered for the valuation postings. Normally, this is left blank.

FASB 52 Tab

In this second step, the valuated Local Currency is translated into Group Currency.

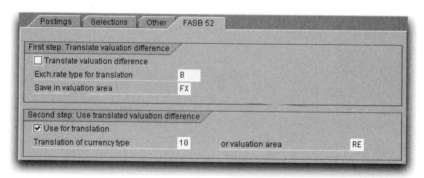

© SAP AG, 2006

- **Translate Valuation Difference.** Not used for revaluation "type 30" (transaction to group). This is used in the first step, revaluation 10 (Transaction to Local Currency).

- **Exchange Rate Type for Translation.** Select the appropriate exchange rate type.

> The exchange rate type for translation must be selected with the same exchange rate used in the "Type 10" revaluation, even during the second step. If this is not done, the revaluation calculations will not be correct.

- **Save in Valuation Area.** Not used for revaluation "type 30" (Transaction to Group Currency). This is used in the first step, revaluation 10 (Transaction to Local Currency).

- **Use for Translation.** Select this to execute the second step of the translation to Group Currency using valuation areas.

- **Translation of Currency Type or Valuation Area.** Select this indicator to store the valuation in valuation area RE.

SAP Execution: Execution

Key date 01/31/05
Valuation in Group currency (30)
Method MEND Month End Valuation Method

G/L acct	Amount in FC	Curr.	Amount grp curr	Amount valuated	Exch.rate	Exch.rate	Ty	Pstg date	Old difference	New difference
140000	72,105.00	EUR	98,116.32	94,068.18	1.30460	1.36074	KR	01/05/2005	0.00	4,048.14-
* 140000		EUR	98,116.32						0.00	4,048.14-
** 140000			98,116.32						0.00	4,048.14-
*** Target Comp. Code UK01			98,116.32						0.00	4,048.14-

© SAP AG, 2006

99

- **Amount in FC.** For group valuation, this is the Local Currency amount in EUR (open item cumulative balance) from the valuation 10 calculation (72,105 EUR in this example).

- **Amount in Group Currency.** This is the open item cumulative balance in Group Currency ($98,116.32 USD in this example). The original Group Currency balance ($96,055.05 USD) is added to the Group Currency translated adjustment amount ($2,061.27 USD) from "Type 10" revaluation.

- **Amount Valuated.** This is the Transaction Currency (72,105 EUR) translated into Group Currency (94,068.18 USD) on key date.

- **Old Difference.** This is the cumulative valuation adjustment that resulted from the most recent valuation.

- **New Difference.** This is the current cumulative valuation adjustment, valuated Group Currency ($94,068.18 USD), less the current period cumulative balance ($98,116.32 USD). The cumulative balance is the original posting in USD plus the translated amount in USD.

SAP Execution: Posting

```
CoCd Doc.no.     Document header text     Type  Pstg date  Curr. Text
Itm PK G/L acct   Text                                     Amount  Amt.in loc.cur.      LC2 amount

UK01             FC valuation SAPF100           01/31/2005 GBP
  1 40 230010      140000 - Valuation by 20050131          0.00           0.00          4,048.14
  2 50 140099      140000 - Valuation by 20050131          0.00           0.00          4,048.14

UK01             Reverse posting SAPF100       02/01/2005 GBP
  1 50 230010      140000 - Valuation by 20050131          0.00           0.00          4,048.14
  2 40 140099      140000 - Valuation by 20050131          0.00           0.00          4,048.14
```

© SAP AG, 2006

- **Local Currency 2 Amount.** This is not relevant in this valuation method "Type 30."

- **Local Currency 2 Amount.** This is the current cumulative valuation adjustment, which is the Group Currency for the current period ($94,068.18 USD), less the cumulative balance ($98,116.32 USD in this example).

- **Process Batch Session.** Run SM35 to process the batch session. Select "Process errors only," and Execute.

SAP Execution: Validation

In order to validate the results, select a few G/L accounts to analyze. Use the following steps to compare the revaluation from Local Currency to Global Currency:

Step 1. Run SAP transaction code FBL3N for the open items on the key date for the same G/L accounts selected, or select a few to review. Exclude the amounts (Transaction Currency) where they are zero so you do not pick up adjustment amounts. Take the Transaction Currency and convert it to the Local Currency using the exchange rate for the key date being used. Take the resulting valuated Local Currency amount and convert it to the Global Currency using the exchange rate for the key date being used.

Step 2. Take the original Global Currency (prior period) and the Global Currency amount calculated by the previous step and compare the SAP calculation, Exhibit 5.4.

Multiple Valuation Areas	Transaction/ Document Currency		Local/ Functional Currency		Group/ Reporting Currency			Exchange Rates	
	Amount	Currency	Amount	Currency	Amount	Currency		GBP/EUR	EUR/USD
5-Jan	50,000.00	GBP	70,525.00	EUR	96,055.05	USD	M-Rate	1.4105	1.36200
31-Jan	50,000.00	GBP	72,105.00	EUR	94,068.18	USD	Spot-Rate	1.4421	1.30460
28-Feb	50,000.00	GBP	72,610.00	EUR	96,193.73	USD	Spot-Rate	1.4522	1.32480

Period 1	Transaction/ Document Currency		Local/ Functional Currency		Group/ Reporting Currency	
	Amount	Currency	Amount	Currency	Amount	Currency
1/31-reval 10	50,000.00	GBP	1,580.00	EUR	2,061.27	USD
1/31 cum.bal.	50,000.00	GBP		EUR	98,116.32	USD
1/31-CTA	50,000.00	GBP		EUR	-4,048.13	USD

Exhibit 5.4 Excel Calculation

REVALUATION "TYPE 10": PERIOD 2 SETUP AND EXECUTION 02/28/2005

In this section, the foreign currency account balances will be revaluated from Transactional Currency (GBP) to Local Currency (EUR). The difference that results from the exchange rate fluctuations on the date of revaluation will be posted in SAP.

Header Data

© SAP AG, 2006

SAP Execution: Execution

Key date 02/28/05
Valuation in Company code currency (10)
Method MEND Month End Valuation Method

G/L acct	Amount in FC	Curr.	Amt.in loc.curr.	Amount valuated	Exch.rate	Exch.rate	Ty	Pstg date	Old difference	New difference
140000	50,000.00	GBP	70,525.00	72,610.00	1.45220	1.41050	KR	01/05/2005	0.00	2,085.00
* 140000		GBP	70,525.00						0.00	2,085.00
** 140000			70,525.00						0.00	2,085.00
*** Target Comp. Code UK01			70,525.00						0.00	2,085.00

- **Amount in FC.** This is the document currency (50,000 GBP in this example).

- **Amount in Local Currency.** This is the open item cumulative balance in Local Currency (70,525 EUR in this example).

- **Amount Valuated.** This is the Transaction Currency (50,000 GBP) translated into Local Currency (72,610 EUR in this example) on the key date.

- **Old Difference.** This is the cumulative valuation adjustment that resulted from the prior valuation.

- **New Difference.** This is the current cumulative valuation adjustment, which is the valuated amount, Transaction Currency translated into EUR on the key date (72,610 EUR), less the Local Currency amount in EUR (70,525 EUR).

SAP Execution: Posting

CoCd Doc.no.	Document header text	Type	Pstg date	Curr.	Text		
Itm PK G/L acct	Text				Amount	Amt.in loc.cur.	LC2 amount
UK01	FC valuation SAPF100		02/28/2005	GBP			
1 50 280010	140000 - Valuation by 20050228				0.00	2,085.00	2,762.21
2 40 140099	140000 - Valuation by 20050228				0.00	2,085.00	2,762.21
UK01	Reverse posting SAPF100		03/01/2005	GBP			
1 40 280010	140000 - Valuation by 20050228				0.00	2,085.00	2,762.21
2 50 140099	140000 - Valuation by 20050228				0.00	2,085.00	2,762.21

© SAP AG, 2006

- **Amount in Local Currency.** This is the difference between the old valuated amount and the new valuated amount.

- **Local Currency 2 Amount.** This is the Local Currency (2,085 EUR) revaluated difference translated into Group Currency ($2,762.21 USD).

- **Process Batch Session.** If a batch session was created, run transaction SM35 to process the batch session. Select "Process errors only," and Execute.

SAP Execution: Validation

In order to validate the results, select a few G/L accounts to analyze. Use the following steps to compare the revaluation from Transaction to Local Currency:

Step 1. Run FBL3N for the open items on the key date for the same G/L accounts selected, or select a few to review. Exclude the amounts (Transaction Currency) where they are zero so you do not pick up adjustment amounts. Take the Transaction Currency and convert it to the Local Currency, using the exchange rate for the key date being used.

Step 2. Take the original Local Currency (prior period) and the Local Currency amount calculated by the previous step and compare the SAP calculation, Exhibit 5.5.

Multiple Valuation Areas

	Transaction/ Document Currency		Local/ Functional Currency		Group/ Reporting Currency			Exchange Rates	
	Amount	Currency	Amount	Currency	Amount	Currency		GBP/EUR	EUR/USD
5-Jan	50,000.00	GBP	70,525.00	EUR	96,055.05	USD	M-Rate	1.4105	1.36200
31-Jan	50,000.00	GBP	72,105.00	EUR	94,068.18	USD	Spot-Rate	1.4421	1.30460
28-Feb	50,000.00	GBP	72,610.00	EUR	96,193.73	USD	Spot-Rate	1.4522	1.32480

Period 2

	Transaction/ Document Currency		Local/ Functional Currency		Group/ Reporting Currency	
	Amount	Currency	Amount	Currency	Amount	Currency
2/28-reval 10	50,000.00	GBP	2,085.00	EUR	2,762.21	USD

Exhibit 5.5   Excel Calculation

REVALUATION "TYPE 30":
PERIOD 2 SETUP AND EXECUTION 02/28/2005

In this section, the foreign currency account balances will be revaluated by taking the difference of the EUR/USD exchange rate for the current period and the original period, times the original Local Currency posting. The difference that results from the exchange rate fluctuations on the date of revaluation will be posted in SAP.

Header Data

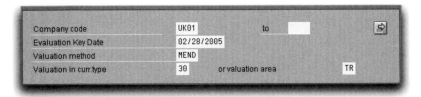

© SAP AG, 2006

SAP Execution: Execution

Key date 02/28/05
Valuation in Group currency (30)
Method MEND Month End Valuation Method

G/L acct	Amount in FC	Curr.	Amount grp curr	Amount valuated	Exch.rate	Exch.rate	Ty	Pstg date	Old difference	New difference
140000	72,610.00	EUR	98,817.26	96,193.73	1.32480	1.36093	KR	01/05/2005	0.00	2,623.53-
* 140000		EUR	98,817.26						0.00	2,623.53-
** 140000			98,817.26						0.00	2,623.53-
*** Target Comp. Code UK01			98,817.26						0.00	2,623.53-

© SAP AG, 2006

- **Amount in FC.** For group valuation, this is the Local Currency amount in EUR (open item cumulative balance) from the valuation 10 calculation (72,610 EUR in this example).

- **Amount in Group Currency.** This is the open item cumulative balance in Group Currency ($98,817.26 USD in this example). The original Group Currency balance ($96,055.05 USD) is added to the Group Currency translated adjustment amount ($2,762.21 USD) from "Type 10" revaluation.

- **Amount Valuated.** This is the Transaction Currency (72,610 EUR) translated into Group Currency (96,193.73 USD) on key date.

- **Old Difference.** This is the cumulative valuation adjustment that resulted from the most recent valuation.

- **New Difference.** This is the current cumulative valuation adjustment, valuated Group Currency ($96,193.73 USD), less the current period cumulative balance ($98,817.26 USD). The cumulative balance is the original posting in USD plus the translated amount in USD.

SAP Execution: Posting

© SAP AG, 2006

- **Local Currency 2 Amount.** This is not relevant in this valuation method "Type 30."

- **Local Currency 2 Amount.** This is the current cumulative valuation adjustment, which is the Group Currency for the current period ($96,193.73 USD), less the cumulative balance ($98,817.26 USD in this example).

- **Process Batch Session.** Run SM35 to process the batch session. Select "Process errors only," and Execute.

SAP Execution: Validation

In order to validate the results, select a few G/L accounts to analyze. Use the following steps to compare the revaluation from Local Currency to Global Currency:

Step 1. Run SAP transaction FBL3N for the open items on the key date for the same G/L accounts selected, or select a few to review. Exclude the amounts (Transaction Currency) where they are zero so you do not pick up adjustment amounts. Take the Transaction Currency and convert it to the Local Currency, using the exchange rate for the key date being used. Take the resulting valuated Local Currency amount and convert it to the Global Currency, using the exchange rate for the key date being used.

Step 2. Take the original Global Currency (prior period) and the Global Currency amount calculated by the previous step and compare the SAP calculation, Exhibit 5.6.

Multiple Valuation Areas	Transaction/ Document Currency		Local/ Functional Currency		Group/ Reporting Currency			Exchange Rates	
	Amount	Currency	Amount	Currency	Amount	Currency		GBP/EUR	EUR/USD
5-Jan	50,000.00	GBP	70,525.00	EUR	96,055.05	USD	M-Rate	1.4105	1.36200
31-Jan	50,000.00	GBP	72,105.00	EUR	94,068.18	USD	Spot-Rate	1.4421	1.30460
28-Feb	50,000.00	GBP	72,610.00	EUR	96,193.73	USD	Spot-Rate	1.4522	1.32480

Period 2	Transaction/ Document Currency		Local/ Functional Currency		Group/ Reporting Currency	
	Amount	Currency	Amount	Currency	Amount	Currency
2/28-reval 10	50,000.00	GBP	2,085.00	EUR	2,762.21	USD
2/28 cum.bal.	50,000.00	GBP		EUR	98,817.26	USD
2/28-CTA	50,000.00	GBP		EUR	−2,623.53	USD

Exhibit 5.6 Excel Calculation

UNIQUE CONFIGURATION

Three tables can be configured for foreign currency revaluation. Only Table V-T030HB (see Exhibit 5.9) is relevant to this chapter "foreign currency revaluation with valuation areas." If it is not configured and revaluation is run, SAP will generate a batch input session to complete the incorrect postings. If it is a realized Gain/Loss posting attempted by SAP and the configuration does not exist, the result will be a hard error.

Table V-T030HB is used to configure the account assignments when using revaluation areas. Note that if the one valuation area method is used, the previous table V-T030H can still be used as the table for account assignments.

DEFINE DEPRECIATION (VALUATION) AREAS

Exhibit 5.7 describes the menu path and transaction code, and Exhibit 5.8 shows it on the menu. Valuation areas are required with this valuation method. Valuation areas store the translated amounts in table BSIS. Valuation areas are freely definable, as in Exhibit 5.9.

	Transaction is Accessed via:
Via Menus	IMG → Financial Accounting → Accts Rec. & Accts Pay. → Business Transactions → Closing → Valuate → Foreign Currency Valuation → Define Depreciation Areas (Exhibit 5.8)
Via Transaction Code	SPRO

Exhibit 5.7   Access Sequence

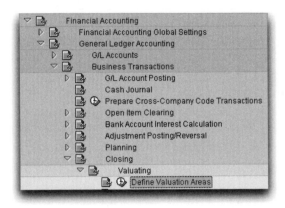

Exhibit 5.8   Menu Path
© SAP AG, 2006

FOREIGN CURRENCY VALUATION: AUTOMATIC POSTINGS

This table should be maintained if postings are made to an open item managed account or reconciliation account managed in a foreign Transaction Currency. Exhibit 5.10 describes the menu path and transaction code, and Exhibit 5.11 shows it on the menu.

Valuation	C.	Long text	Add. cur...	Add. cur...
FX	30	Reval LC to GC TEMP Difference		
RE	10	Cocode Curr. Reval 10		
TR	30	GC Translation		

- **RE.** Represents the Local Currency, and is used in the header section of the valuation run to store the Local Currency difference.
- **FX.** Represents Group Currency, and is used for temporarily storing the first steps (local to group translation difference) of the valuation in the FASB 52 tab.
- **TR.** Represents Group Currency, and is used in the second section of the FASB 52 tab. This can contain the translation differences but is primarily used for account determination in the configuration table.

Exhibit 5.9   Define FI Valuation Areas
© SAP AG, 2006

	Transaction is Accessed via:
Via Menus	IMG → Financial Accounting → Accts Rec. & Accts Pay. → Business Transactions → Closing → Valuate → Foreign Currency Valuation → Prepare Automatic Posting for Foreign Currency Valuation (Exhibit 5.11)
Via Transaction Code	OBA1

Exhibit 5.10   Access Sequence

The table in Exhibit 5.12 allows for configuring non–open items and open item accounts using full valuation areas. Select the Chart of Accounts (e.g., INT) to configure the G/L accounts. Select the yellow arrow to transition to the valuation area screen.

Select the valuation area to assign G/L accounts to in Exhibit 5.13. Valuation RE will have G/L accounts assigned to it for revaluation "Type 10" Transaction to Local Currency valuation.

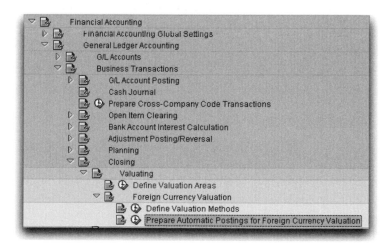

Exhibit 5.11   Menu Path
© SAP AG, 2006

Maintain FI Configuration: Automatic Posting - Procedures

Group   FWA   Exchange rate differences

Procedures

Description	Transactn	Account determ.
Exch.rate diff. in forgn.curr.balances	KDB	☑
Exchange rate difference in open items	KDF	☑
Payment difference for altern.currency	KDW	☑
Payment diff.for altern.curr.(offset)	KDZ	☑
Internal currencies rounding differences	RDF	☑

Enter Chart of Accounts

Chart of accounts   INT

Exhibit 5.12   Define FI Valuation Area Automatic Account Assignments
© SAP AG, 2006

Enter the G/L account, specific currency (if desired), and then assign the balance sheet adjustment account and the Gain/Loss Account as in Exhibit 5.14.

Select the valuation area to assign G/L accounts to in Exhibit 5.15. Valuation TR will have G/L accounts assigned to it for revaluation "Type 30" Local Currency to Group Currency valuation.

Enter the G/L account, specific currency (if desired), and then assign the balance sheet adjustment account and the Gain/Loss Account as in Exhibit 5.16.

Change valuation area

Valuation area   RE

Exhibit 5.13   Set Depreciation Area to Configure
© SAP AG, 2006

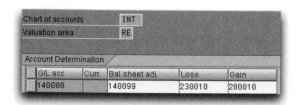

Exhibit 5.14 Configure G/L Accounts per Depreciation/Valuation Area
© SAP AG, 2006

Exhibit 5.15 Set Depreciation Area to Configure
© SAP AG, 2006

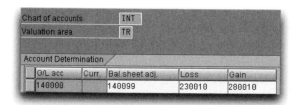

Exhibit 5.16 Configure G/L Accounts per Depreciation/Valuation Area
© SAP AG, 2006

6

REVALUATION WITH ONE VALUATION AREA

HIGHLIGHTS

- Revaluation "Type 10": Period 1 Setup and Execution
- Revaluation "Type 30": Period 1 Setup and Execution
- Revaluation "Type 10": Period 2 Setup and Execution
- Revaluation "Type 30": Period 2 Setup and Execution
- Unique Configuration

This method revaluates the G/L accounts using only one valuation area. The end result is a revaluated balance from Transaction Currency to Local Currency with the Gain/Loss posting as well as with translation and associated Cumulative Translation Adjustment (CTA) posting.

Additionally, postings are done in *full* each time revaluation is run. Reversals are done in *full* prior to each revaluation run.

This method does provide for translation, and allows the original open item table to continue to be used for account assignment postings (T030H). This method of execution has the most benefits.

This is the minimal configuration required to be FASB 52 compliant and still configure the primary account assignment table (V-T030H), as opposed to having to configure the valuation area table (V-T030HB).

> FASB 52 usage in SAP requires at a minimum *one* valuation area to be defined as in this section. Without the use of *at least one* valuation area, the FASB 52 functionality will not work.

	Transaction is Accessed via:
Via Menus	Accounting → Financial Accounting → General Ledger → Periodic Processing → Closing → Valuate → Foreign Currency Valuation (Exhibit 6.2)
Via Transaction Code	F.05

Exhibit 6.1   Access Sequence

SAP provides a means to execute foreign currency revaluation on specific G/L accounts managed in foreign currencies (Exhibit 6.1). Exhibit 6.1 describes the menu path and transaction code, and Exhibit 6.2 shows it on the menu. Transaction code F.05 allows the revaluation of one or more accounts at the same time. The following steps occur with currency revaluation execution:

Step 1. Each G/L account's line item selected is revalued using the exchange rate of the key evaluation date.

Exhibit 6.2   Menu Path
© SAP AG, 2006

Step 2. A posting is generated to the appropriate unrealized Gain/Loss account and balance statement adjustment account.

Step 3. A reversal posting is generated in total for the next day (unless you specify another date) to reverse the postings to the unrealized Gain/Loss.

Currency revaluation has various configurations that are required:

- Exchange rate types are set up.
- Valuation methods are set up (OB59).
- Document types are set up (OBA7).
- Exchange rates are entered for each currency (OC41).
- Account determination has been defined (OBA1).
- Posting keys are assigned for adjustment postings.

REVALUATION "TYPE 10": PERIOD 1 SETUP AND EXECUTION 1/31/2005

In this section, the foreign currency account balances will be revaluated by converting the Transaction Currency posting (GBP) to Local Currency (EUR) using the exchange rate for the original posting and the Transaction Currency posting (GBP) to Local Currency (EUR) using the exchange rate for the evaluation key date. The difference that results from the exchange rate fluctuations on the date of revaluation will be posted in SAP.

Header Area

© SAP AG, 2006

- **Company Code.** Select the company code or company codes that are to be revaluated. Some companies prefer to centralize this function, whereas other companies decentralize it. Either way, you can run it for one or more company codes at the same time. It depends on how you want to analyze the output.

> When you run this for multiple company codes, the G/L accounts that are selected for revaluation are run for all companies selected. For example, a specific G/L account (e.g., 2050) might exist in all company codes, but revaluation runs might only be desired in one or a select number of company codes. If company codes have different G/Ls that require revaluation, it might be best to run the company codes separately.

- **Evaluation Key Date.** The evaluation key date is used to determine the date of the currency exchange rates used in the revaluation. SAP will look for the exchange rate that falls on the key date entered. If one does not exist for that specific date, it will look for the exchange rate for the closest date prior to the date entered as the evaluation key date. The evaluation key date should be the last day of the period.

  The evaluation key date is also used to evaluate open item documents that have not been cleared as of this date (periods 13 through 16 are considered if the key date is within periods 1 through 12).

- **Valuation Method.** Valuation method is the key that determines a foreign currency valuation method/approach used when carrying out the foreign currency revaluation. The most important field read from the valuation method is the type of exchange rate used (average or spot). Refer to the common configuration area to read more information specific to this key.

- **Valuation in Currency Type or Valuation Area.** Valuation currency type defines the type of valuation being performed. First Local Currency for valuation defines the Currency Type for Transactional Currency to Local Currency valuation ("Type 10" in these examples).

Postings Tab

© SAP AG, 2006

- **Balance Sheet Preparation Valuation.** This parameter can only be used for valuation runs that do not use valuation areas. This indicator does not have an effect on non–open item accounts; it only affects open item accounts.

    For open item accounts, this indicator is key. If *not* selected, reversals will be posted and valuation will be cumulative. If selected, no reversal postings will occur and valuation will be incremental. Refer to SAP Note No. 87538 in the References section at the end of the book. Most companies that run revaluation via this method (e.g., not using valuation areas) do not reverse postings and post incrementally.

    To post reversals for non–open item accounts, select the "reverse postings" indicator at the bottom under "For G/L Account Balance Valuation" and choose a date. To post reversals for both open item and non–open item accounts, do not select the "balance sheet preparation valuation" indicator and select the "reverse postings" indicator at the bottom.

- **Create Postings.** Leave this indicator blank to run the valuation in test mode. Select the indicator to make the postings in FI. When selected, the postings can either be executed immediately in the foreground, in the background, or a batch input session can be specified.

- **Batch Input Session Name.** If you enter a name here, a batch input session with that name will be created. Transaction SM35 must be used to process the batch session. The postings will not be made until the batch session is processed. If you do not enter a name here, the postings will be made immediately.

- **Document Date.** The document date of the unrealized postings can be specified here or SAP will default to the valuation key date.
- **Posting Date.** The posting date of the unrealized postings can be specified here or SAP will default to the valuation key date.
- **Posting Period.** Posting period in which the valuation postings are generated. The number entered should correspond to the period that includes the posting date or valuation key date.
- **Reversal Posting Date.** The posting date of the reversal postings can be specified here; otherwise, SAP will default to the next day. This is normally the first day of the next period or the next day if running valuation daily. This is for non–open item accounts only.
- **Reversal Posting Period.** This is the posting period in which the valuation postings are generated. This must correspond to the posting date. This is for non–open item accounts only.
- **Reverse Postings.** This indicator affects the valuation of non–open items only. If not selected, the G/L balances for non–open item accounts will not be reversed. If selected, they will be reversed in full.

Selections Tab

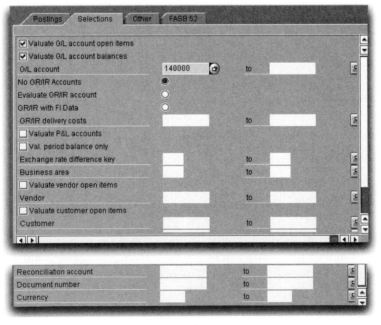

© SAP AG, 2006

- **Valuate G/L Account Open Items.** Select this indicator in combination with identifying the specific open item G/L accounts to be valuated.

- **Valuate G/L Account Balances.** Select this indicator in combination with identifying the specific G/L balance accounts to be valuated.

- **G/L Account.** Identify the specific open item G/L account(s) that will be revaluated. These same G/L accounts will appear in the G/L balance tab, and even if the "Valuate G/L Account Open Items" indicator is selected, the accounts identified in both the open items and G/L balance tab will be valuated based on their G/L account definition as open item or line item. If a range of G/L accounts that include both open item and non–open item accounts is identified, and only the "Valuate G/L Account Open Items" indicator is selected, then only the G/L accounts in the range that are open item will be revaluated.

- **No GR/IR Accounts.** If selected, no GR/IR valuation will occur. GR/IR should be revaluated.

- **Evaluate GR/IR Accounts.** If selected, open items with a goods receipt (MIGO) will be valuated in the GR/IR account. The Purchase Order Currency is then valuated. The valuation is only completed if the goods receipt has occurred, because this is when the first financial posting occurs. The GR/IR account is an open item account, and postings will automatically be reversed. Revaluation occurs based on the Purchase Order Currency. Refer to SAP Note No. 441333 in the References for more information.

- **GR/IR with FI Data.** If you select this indicator, revaluation will occur on *all* items in the GR/IR account. U.S. clients may choose to use this field as opposed to the previous field because this gives more control to the person running the revaluation.

- **GR/IR Delivery Costs.** Specify accounts for GR/IR transaction cost postings. Transactions with debit balances (invoices without goods) should not be valuated. The vendor invoice will be valuated. Goods delivered but not invoiced will be valuated with this indicator setting.

- **Valuate P&L Accounts.** Select to valuate P&L accounts. This is not normally selected unless fixed asset depreciation is being revaluated. Do not reverse P&L postings.

- **Valuate Period Balance Only.** This is not normally selected unless running revaluation on P&L accounts. Selecting this indicator valuates the period balance and not the cumulative balance.

- **Exchange Rate Difference Key.** If exchange rate difference keys are utilized on G/L account master data for non–open item accounts, this field can be used to uniquely identify the valuation for specific exchange rate keys.

- **Business Area.** Revaluation can be run for specific business areas (if business areas are used).

- **Valuate Vendor Open Items.** To valuate vendor (payables) open items, select this indicator and select the appropriate vendors or range of vendors in the next field.

- **Vendor.** Select the vendor(s) or range of vendors to valuate along with the previous indicator "Value Vendor Open Items."

- **Valuate Customer Open Items.** To valuate customer (receivable) open items, select this indicator and select the appropriate customers or range of customers in the next field.

- **Customer.** Select the customer(s) or range of customers to valuate, along with the previous indicator "Valuate Customer Open Items."

- **Reconciliation Account.** This field can be used as an alternative to listing the vendors or customers. The vendor or customer reconciliation accounts are listed here. If used, only vendors (or customers) assigned to this G/L reconciliation account(s) will be valuated.

- **Document Number.** This is used to select one or more specific documents for valuation. This is not normally used for production runs but is useful in testing valuation so that valuation and postings are kept to a specific document test.

- **Currency.** Valuation runs can be limited to execution by currency. To run revaluation on just GBP currency, enter this information. Leaving this field blank will select all open items for valuation for any currency.

- **SL Extra.** Split ledger functionality in SAP R/3 v4.7 allows you to distribute valuation differences to profit centers or business areas based on how the split ledger ZZPLIT is set up.

Other Tab

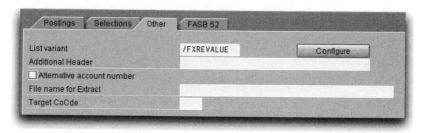

© SAP AG, 2006

- **List Variant.** The list variant is useful in displaying all of the balances SAP uses to calculate the valuation postings.

- **Additional Header.** A report header/description can be entered here, and it will be entered on the valuation report.

- **Alternative Account Number.** If selected, the alternative account number defined on the G/L account master record is used. This is normally used if a country chart of accounts is maintained in the company codes selected. Remember that the financial statements will need to be updated to include the alternative accounts. Normally, this is not selected.

- **File Name for Extract.** Enter a file name if an extract is desired. Otherwise, leave this field blank.

- **Target Co-code.** A cross-company code can be entered for the valuation postings. Normally, this is left blank.

FASB 52 Tab

In this first step, foreign currency Transaction Currency items are valuated and posted to P&L accounts in the Local Currency. Additionally, the valuation difference is translated into Group Currency and posted. The difference that is translated into Group Currency is stored in the valuation area FX.

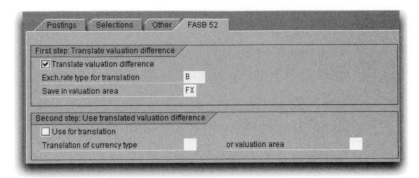

- **Translate Valuation Difference.** Select this indicator to execute the translation using valuation areas.

- **Exchange Rate Type for Translation.** Select the appropriate exchange rate type.

- **Save in Valuation Area.** Select this indicator to store the valuation in valuation area FX.

- **Use for Translation.** This is not used for revaluation "Type 10" (Transaction to Local Currency). This is used for the second step, revaluation 30 (Transaction to Group Currency).

- **Translation of Currency Type or Valuation Area.** This is not used for revaluation "Type 10" (Transaction to Local Currency). This is used for the second step, revaluation 30 (Transaction to Group Currency).

SAP Execution: Execution

Key date 01/31/05
Valuation in Company code currency (10)
Method MEND Month End Valuation Method

G/L acct.	Amount in FC	Curr.	Amt.in loc.cur.	Amount valuated	Exch.rate	Exch.rate	Ty	Pstg date	Old difference	New difference
140000	50,000.00	GBP	70,525.00	72,105.00	1.44210	1.41050	KR	01/05/2005	0.00	1,580.00
* 140000		GBP	70,525.00						0.00	1,580.00
** 140000			70,525.00						0.00	1,580.00
*** Target Comp. Code UK01			70,525.00						0.00	1,580.00

- **Amount in FC.** This is the document currency (50,000 GBP in this example).

- **Amount in Local Currency.** This is the open item cumulative balance in Local Currency (70,525 EUR in this example).

- **Amount Valuated.** This is the Transaction Currency (50,000 GBP) translated into Local Currency (72,105 EUR) on the key date.

- **Old Difference.** This is the cumulative valuation adjustment that resulted from the prior valuation.

- **New Difference.** This is the current cumulative valuation adjustment, which is the valuated amount, Transaction Currency translated into EUR on the key date (72,105 EUR), less the Local Currency amount in EUR (70,525 EUR).

SAP Execution: Posting

```
CoCd Doc.no.     Document header text     Type  Pstg date  Curr. Text
Itm PK G/L acct  Text                                Amount  Amt.in loc.cur.    LC2 amount

UK01 100000016  FC valuation SAPF100          01/31/2005 GBP
  1 50 280010     140000 - Valuation by 20050131         0.00        1,580.00       2,061.27
  2 40 140099     140000 - Valuation by 20050131         0.00        1,580.00       2,061.27

UK01 100000017  Reverse posting SAPF100       02/01/2005 GBP
  1 40 280010     140000 - Valuation by 20050131         0.00        1,580.00       2,061.27
  2 50 140099     140000 - Valuation by 20050131         0.00        1,580.00       2,061.27
```

© SAP AG, 2006

- **Amount in Local Currency.** This is the difference between the old valuated amount and the new valuated amount.

- **Local Currency 2 Amount.** This is the Local Currency (1,580 EUR) revaluated difference translated into Group Currency ($2,061.27 USD).

- **Process Batch Session.** Run SM35 to process the batch session. Select "Process errors only," and Execute.

SAP Execution: Validation

In order to validate the results, select a few G/L accounts to analyze. Use the following steps to compare the revaluation from Transaction to Local Currency:

Step 1. Run SAP transaction code FBL3N for the open items on the key date for the same G/L accounts selected, or select a few to review. Exclude the amounts (Transaction Currency) where they are zero so you do not pick up adjustment amounts. Take the Transaction Currency and convert it to the Local Currency, using the exchange rate for the key date being used.

Step 2. Take the original Local Currency (prior period) and the Local Currency amount calculated by the previous step and compare the SAP calculation, Exhibit 6.3.

One Valuation Area	Transaction/ Document Currency		Local/ Functional Currency		Group/ Reporting Currency			Exchange Rates	
	Amount	Currency	Amount	Currency	Amount	Currency		GBP/EUR	EUR/USD
5-Jan	50,000.00	GBP	70,525.00	EUR	96,055.05	USD	M-Rate	1.4105	1.36200
31-Jan	50,000.00	GBP	72,105.00	EUR	94,068.18	USD	Spot-Rate	1.4421	1.30460
28-Feb	50,000.00	GBP	72,610.00	EUR	96,193.73	USD	Spot-Rate	1.4522	1.32480

Period 1	Transaction/ Document Currency		Local/ Functional Currency		Group/ Reporting Currency	
	Amount	Currency	Amount	Currency	Amount	Currency
1/31-reval 10	50,000.00	GBP	1,580.00	EUR	2,061.27	USD

Exhibit 6.3   Excel Calculation

132

REVALUATION "TYPE 30": PERIOD 1 SETUP AND EXECUTION 1/31/2005

In this section, the cumulative balance is calculated by taking the revaluated amount from the revaluation "Type 10" calculation, translated into Group Currency, and adding the original Group Currency translated balance. The difference between this amount and Group Currency translated on the key date is the cumulative translation adjustment posted in SAP.

Header Information

© SAP AG, 2006

- **Company Code.** Select the company code or company codes that are to be revaluated. Some companies prefer to centralize this function, whereas other companies decentralize it. Either way, you can run it for one or more company codes at the same time. It depends on how you want to analyze the output.

> When you run this for multiple company codes, the G/L accounts that are selected for revaluation are run for all companies selected. For example, a specific G/L account (e.g., 2050) might exist in all company codes, but revaluation runs might only be desired in one or a select number of company codes. If company codes have different G/Ls that require revaluation, it might be best to run the company codes separately.

- **Evaluation Key Date.** The evaluation key date is used to determine the date of the currency exchange rates used in the revaluation. SAP will look for the exchange rate that falls on the key date entered. If one does not exist for that specific date, it will look for the exchange rate for the closest date prior to the date entered as the evaluation key date. The evaluation key date should be the last day of the period.

The evaluation key date is also used to evaluate open item documents that have not been cleared as of this date (periods 13 through 16 are considered if the key date is within periods 1 through 12).

- **Valuation Method.** Valuation method is the key that determines a foreign currency valuation method/approach used when carrying out the foreign currency revaluation. The most important field read from the valuation method is the type of exchange rate used (average or spot). Refer to the common configuration area to read more information specific to this key.

- **Valuation in Currency Type or Valuation Area.** Valuation currency type defines the type of valuation being performed. Second Local Currency type defined for valuation defines the Currency Type for Local Currency to Group Currency valuation ("Type 30" in these examples).

Postings Tab

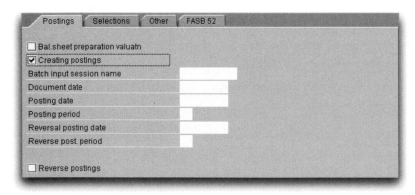

© SAP AG, 2006

- **Balance Sheet Preparation Valuation.** This parameter can only be used for valuation runs that do not use valuation areas. This indicator does not have an effect on non–open item accounts; it only affects open item accounts.

For open item accounts, this indicator is key. If *not* selected, reversals will be posted and valuation will be cumulative. If selected, no reversal postings will occur and valuation will be incremental. Refer to SAP Note No. 87538 in the References. Most companies that run revaluation via this method (e.g., not using valuation areas) do not reverse postings and post incrementally.

To post reversals for non–open item accounts, select the "reverse postings" indicator at the bottom under "For G/L Account Balance Valuation" and choose a date. To post reversals for both open item and non–open item accounts, do not select the "balance sheet preparation" valuation indicator, and select the "reverse postings" indicator at the bottom.

- **Create Postings.** Leave this indicator blank to run the valuation in test mode. Select the indicator to make the postings in FI. When selected, the postings can either be executed immediately in the foreground, in the background, or a batch input session can be specified.

- **Batch Input Session Name.** If you enter a name here, a batch input session with that name will be created. Transaction SM35 must be used to process the batch session. The postings will not be made until the batch session is processed. If you do not enter a name here, the postings will be made immediately.

- **Document Date.** The document date of the unrealized postings can be specified here or SAP will default to the valuation key date.

- **Posting Date.** The posting date of the unrealized postings can be specified here or SAP will default to the valuation key date.

- **Posting Period.** Posting period in which the valuation postings are generated. The number entered should correspond to the period that includes the posting date or valuation key date.

- **Reversal Posting Date.** The posting date of the reversal postings can be specified here; otherwise, SAP will default to the next day. This is normally the first day of the next period or the next day if running valuation daily. This is for non–open item accounts only.

- **Reversal Posting Period.** This is the posting period in which the valuation postings are generated. This must correspond to the posting date. This is for non–open item accounts only.

- **Reverse Postings.** This indicator affects the valuation of non–open items only. If not selected, the G/L balances for non–open item accounts will not be reversed. If selected, they will be reversed in full.

Selections Tab

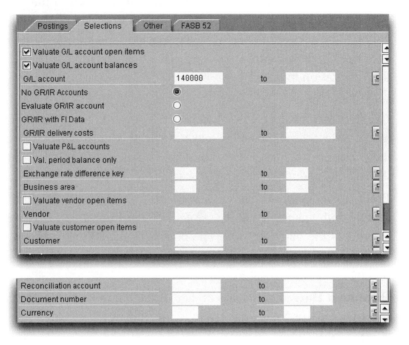

© SAP AG, 2006

- **Valuate G/L Account Open Items.** Select this indicator in combination with identifying the specific open item G/L accounts to be valuated.

- **Valuate G/L Account Balances.** Select this indicator in combination with identifying the specific G/L balance accounts to be valuated.

- **G/L Account.** Identify the specific open item G/L account(s) that will be revaluated. These same G/L accounts will appear in the G/L balance tab, and even if the "Valuate G/L Account Open Items" indicator is selected, the accounts identified in both the open items and G/L balance tab will be valuated based on their G/L account definition as open item or line item. If a range of G/L accounts that include both open item and non–open item accounts is identified, and only the "Valuate G/L Account Open Items" indicator is selected, then only the G/L accounts in the range that are open item will be revaluated.

- **No GR/IR Accounts.** If selected, no GR/IR valuation will occur. GR/IR should be revaluated.

- **Evaluate GR/IR Accounts.** If selected, open items with a goods receipt (MIGO) will be valuated in the GR/IR account. The Purchase Order Currency is then valuated. The valuation is only completed if the goods receipt has occurred, because this is when the first financial posting occurs. The GR/IR account is an open item account, and postings will automatically be reversed. Revaluation occurs based on the Purchase Order Currency. Refer to SAP Note No. 441333 in the References for more information.

- **GR/IR with FI Data.** If you select this indicator, revaluation will occur on *all* items in the GR/IR account. U.S. clients may choose to use this field as opposed to the previous field because this gives more control to the person running the revaluation.

- **GR/IR Delivery Costs.** Specify accounts for GR/IR transaction cost postings. Transactions with debit balances (invoices without goods) should not be valuated. The vendor invoice will be valuated. Goods delivered but not invoiced will be valuated with this indicator setting.

- **Valuate P&L Accounts.** Select to valuate P&L accounts. This is not normally selected unless fixed asset depreciation is being revaluated. Do not reverse P&L postings.

- **Valuate Period Balance Only.** This is not normally selected unless running revaluation on P&L accounts. Selecting this indicator valuates the period balance and not the cumulative balance.

- **Exchange Rate Difference Key.** If exchange rate difference keys are utilized on G/L account master data for non–open item accounts, this field can be used to uniquely identify the valuation for specific exchange rate keys.

- **Business Area.** Revaluation can be run for specific business areas (if business areas are used).

- **Valuate Vendor Open Items.** To valuate vendor (payables) open items, select this indicator and select the appropriate vendors or range of vendors in the next field.

- **Vendor.** Select the vendor(s) or range of vendors to valuate along with the previous indicator "Value Vendor Open Items."

- **Valuate Customer Open Items.** To valuate customer (receivable) open items, select this indicator and select the appropriate customers or range of customers in the next field.

- **Customer.** Select the customer(s) or range of customers to valuate, along with the previous indicator "Valuate Customer Open Items."

- **Reconciliation Account.** This field can be used as an alternative to listing the vendors or customers. The vendor or customer reconciliation accounts are listed here. If used, only vendors (or customers) assigned to this G/L reconciliation account(s) will be valuated.

- **Document Number.** This is used to select one or more specific documents for valuation. This is not normally used for production runs but is useful in testing valuation so that valuation and postings are kept to a specific document test.

- **Currency.** Valuations runs can be limited to execution by currency. To run revaluation on just GBP currency, enter this information. Leaving this field blank will select all open items for valuation for any currency.

- **SL Extra.** Split ledger functionality in SAP R/3 v4.7 allows you to distribute valuation differences to profit centers or business areas based on how the split ledger ZZPLIT is set up.

Other Tab

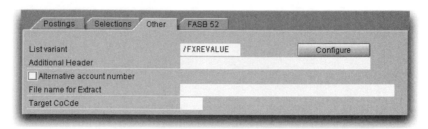

© SAP AG, 2006

- **List Variant.** The list variant is useful in displaying all of the balances SAP uses to calculate the valuation postings.

- **Additional Header.** A report header/description can be entered here, and it will be entered on the valuation report.

- **Alternative Account Number.** If selected, the alternative account number defined on the G/L account master record is used. This is normally used if a country chart of accounts is maintained in the company codes selected. Remember that the financial statements will need to be updated to include the alternative accounts. Normally, this is not selected.

- **File Name for Extract.** Enter a file name if an extract is desired. Otherwise, leave this field blank.

- **Target Co-code.** A cross-company code can be entered for the valuation postings. Normally, this is left blank.

FASB 52 Tab

In this second step, the valuated Local Currency is translated into Group Currency.

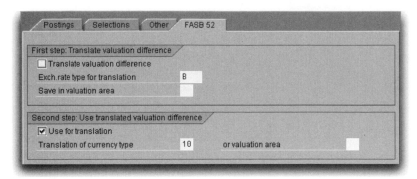

- **Translate Valuation Difference.** This step is not used for revaluation "Type 30" (Transaction to Group Currency). This is used in the first step, revaluation 10 (Transaction to Local Currency).

- **Exchange Rate Type for Translation.** Select the appropriate exchange rate type.

> The exchange rate type for translation must be selected with the same exchange rate type used in the "Type 10" revaluation, even during the second step. If this is not, the revaluation calculations will not be correct.

- **Save in Valuation Area.** This is not used for revaluation "Type 30" (Transaction to Group Currency). This is used in the first step, revaluation 10 (Transaction to Local Currency).

- **Use for Translation.** Select this to execute the second step of the translation to Group Currency using valuation areas.

- **Translation of Currency Type or Valuation Area.** Not required when using one valuation area.

SAP Execution: Execution

Key date 01/31/05
Valuation in Group currency (30)
Method MEND Month End Valuation Method

G/L acct	Amount in FC	Curr.	Amount grp curr.	Amount valuated	Exch.rate	Exch.rate	Ty	Pstg date	Old difference	New difference
140000	70,525.00	EUR	96,055.05	92,006.92	1.30460	1.36200	KR	01/05/2005	0.00	4,048.13-
* 140000		EUR	96,055.05						0.00	4,048.13-
** 140000			96,055.05						0.00	4,048.13-
*** Target Comp. Code UK01			96,055.05						0.00	4,048.13-

© SAP AG, 2006

- **Amount in FC.** For group valuation, this is the Local Currency amount in EUR (open item cumulative balance) from the valuation 10 calculation (70,525 EUR in this example).

- **Amount in Group Currency.** This is the open item cumulative balance in Group Currency ($96,055.05 USD in this example).

- **Amount Valuated.** This is the Transaction Currency (72,105 EUR) translated into Group Currency ($94,068.18 USD) on the key date, less the translated Group Currency amount from "Type 10" valuation ($2,061.27 USD); $92,006.92 USD is the valuated amount in this example.

- **Old Difference.** This is the cumulative valuation adjustment that resulted from the most recent valuation.

- **New Difference.** This is the current cumulative valuation adjustment, which is the open item cumulative balance in Global Currency (96,055.05 USD), less the valuated amount ($92,006.92 USD) (First Local Currency translated to USD).

SAP Execution: Posting

```
CoCd Doc.no.    Document header text    Type  Pstg date  Curr. Text
Itm PK G/L acct  Text                                    Amount  Amt.in loc.cur.    LC2 amount

UK01 100000018  FC valuation SAPF100          01/31/2005 GBP
  1 40 230010     140000 - Valuation by 20050131          0.00           0.00        4,048.13
  2 50 140099     140000 - Valuation by 20050131          0.00           0.00        4,048.13

UK01 100000019  Reverse posting SAPF100       02/01/2005 GBP
  1 50 230010     140000 - Valuation by 20050131          0.00           0.00        4,048.13
  2 40 140099     140000 - Valuation by 20050131          0.00           0.00        4,048.13
```

© SAP AG, 2006

- **Local Currency 2 Amount.** The original Group Currency less the valuated amount.

- **Process Batch Session.** Run SM35 to process the batch session. Select "Process errors only," and select "Execute."

SAP Execution: Validation

In order to validate the results, select a few G/L accounts to analyze. Use the following steps to compare the revaluation from Transaction to Local Currency:

Step 1. Run FBL3N for the open items on the key date for the same G/L accounts selected, or select a few to review. Exclude the Amounts (Transaction Currency) where they are zero so you do not pick up adjustment amounts. Take the Transaction Currency and convert it to the Local Currency using the exchange rate for the key date being used.

Step 2. Take the original Local Currency (prior period) and the Local Currency amount calculated by the previous step and compare the SAP calculation, Exhibit 6.4.

One Valuation Area	Transaction/ Document Currency		Local/ Functional Currency		Group/ Reporting Currency			Exchange Rates	
	Amount	Currency	Amount	Currency	Amount	Currency		GBP/EUR	EUR/USD
5-Jan	50,000.00	GBP	70,525.00	EUR	96,055.05	USD	M-Rate	1.4105	1.36200
31-Jan	50,000.00	GBP	72,105.00	EUR	94,068.18	USD	Spot-Rate	1.4421	1.30460
28-Feb	50,000.00	GBP	72,610.00	EUR	96,193.73	USD	Spot-Rate	1.4522	1.32480

Period 1	Transaction/ Document Currency		Local/ Functional Currency		Group/ Reporting Currency	
	Amount	Currency	Amount	Currency	Amount	Currency
1/31-reval 10	50,000.00	GBP	1,580.00	EUR	2,061.27	USD
1/31 cum.bal.	50,000.00	GBP		EUR	92,006.92	USD
1/31-CTA	50,000.00	GBP		EUR	–4,048.13	USD

Exhibit 6.4 Excel Calculation

If foreign currency revaluation is run with multiple company codes and any of the G/L accounts being run in the same valuation mixed definitions between open item and non–open item, then SAP will use the specifications in this table and ignore any configuration in the previous table V-T030.

REVALUATION "TYPE 10": PERIOD 2 SETUP AND EXECUTION 2/28/2005

In this section, the foreign currency account balances will be revaluated from Transactional Currency (GBP) to Local Currency (EUR). The difference that results from the exchange rate fluctuations on the date of revaluation will be posted in SAP.

Header Area

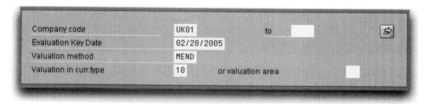

© SAP AG, 2006

SAP Execution: Execution

Key date 02/28/05
Valuation in Company code currency (10)
Method MEND Month End Valuation Method

G/L acct	Amount in FC	Curr.	Amt.in loc.curr.	Amount valuated	Exch.rate	Exch.rate	Ty	Pstg date	Old difference	New difference
140000	50,000.00	GBP	70,525.00	72,610.00	1.45220	1.41050	KR	01/05/2005	0.00	2,085.00
* 140000		GBP	70,525.00						0.00	2,085.00
** 140000			70,525.00						0.00	2,085.00
*** Target Comp. Code UK01			70,525.00						0.00	2,085.00

© SAP AG, 2006

- **Amount in FC.** This is the document currency (50,000 GBP in this example).

- **Amount in Local Currency.** This is the open item cumulative balance in Local Currency (70,525 EUR in this example).

- **Amount Valuated.** This is the Transaction Currency (50,000 GBP) translated into Local Currency (72,610 EUR) on key date.

- **Old Difference.** This is the cumulative valuation adjustment that resulted from the prior valuation.

- **New Difference.** This is the current cumulative valuation adjustment, which is the valuated amount, Transaction Currency translated into EUR on the key date (72,610 EUR), less the Local Currency amount in EUR (70,525 EUR).

SAP Execution: Postings

CoCd Doc.no.	Document header text	Type	Pstg date	Curr. Text			
Itm PK G/L acct	Text			Amount	Amt.in loc.cur.		LC2 amount
UK01 100000020	FC valuation SAPF100		02/28/2005 GBP				
1 50 280010	140000 - Valuation by 20050228			0.00	2,085.00		2,762.21
2 40 140099	140000 - Valuation by 20050228			0.00	2,085.00		2,762.21
UK01 100000021	Reverse posting SAPF100		03/01/2005 GBP				
1 40 280010	140000 - Valuation by 20050228			0.00	2,085.00		2,762.21
2 50 140099	140000 - Valuation by 20050228			0.00	2,085.00		2,762.21

© SAP AG, 2006

- **Amount in Local Currency.** This is the difference between the old valuated amount and the new valuated amount.

- **Local Currency 2 Amount.** This is the Local Currency (2,085 EUR) revaluated difference translated into Group Currency ($2,762.21 USD).

- **Process Batch Session.** If a batch session was created, run transaction SM35 to process the batch session. Select "Process errors only," and Execute.

SAP Execution: Validation

In order to validate the results, select a few G/L accounts to analyze. Use the following steps to compare the revaluation from Transaction to Local Currency:

Step 1. Run FBL3N for the open items on the key date for the same G/L accounts selected, or select a few to review. Exclude the amounts (Transaction Currency) where they are zero so you do not pick up adjustment amounts. Take the Transaction Currency and convert it to the Local Currency, using the exchange rate for the key date being used.

Step 2. Take the original Local Currency (prior period) and the Local Currency amount calculated by the previous step and compare the SAP calculation, Exhibit 6.5.

One Valuation Area	Transaction/ Document Currency		Local/ Functional Currency		Group/ Reporting Currency				Exchange Rates	
	Amount	Currency	Amount	Currency	Amount	Currency			GBP/EUR	EUR/USD
5-Jan	50,000.00	GBP	70,525.00	EUR	96,055.05	USD	M-Rate		1.4105	1.36200
31-Jan	50,000.00	GBP	72,105.00	EUR	94,068.18	USD	Spot-Rate		1.4421	1.30460
28-Feb	50,000.00	GBP	72,610.00	EUR	96,193.73	USD	Spot-Rate		1.4522	1.32480

Period 2	Transaction/ Document Currency		Local/ Functional Currency		Group/ Reporting Currency	
	Amount	Currency	Amount	Currency	Amount	Currency
2/28-reval 10	50,000.00	GBP	2,085.00	EUR	2,762.21	USD

Exhibit 6.5 Excel Calculation

SAP FOREIGN CURRENCY REVALUATION

REVALUATION "TYPE 30":
PERIOD 2 SETUP AND EXECUTION 2/28/2005

In this section, the foreign currency account balances will be revaluated by taking the difference of the EUR/USD exchange rate for the current period and the original period, times the original Local Currency posting. The difference that results from the exchange rate fluctuations on the date of revaluation will be posted in SAP.

Header Information

© SAP AG, 2006

150

SAP Execution: Execution

Key date 02/28/05
Valuation in Group currency (30)
Method MEND Month End Valuation Method

G/L acct	Amount in FC	Curr.	Amount grp curr.	Amount valuated	Exch rate	Exch rate	Ty	Pstg date	Old difference	New difference
140000	70,525.00	EUR	96,055.05	93,431.52	1.32480	1.36200	KR	01/05/2005	0.00	2,623.53-
* 140000		EUR	96,055.05						0.00	2,623.53-
** 140000			96,055.05						0.00	2,623.53-
*** Target Comp. Code UK01			96,055.05						0.00	2,623.53-

- **Amount in FC.** For group valuation, this is the Local Currency amount in EUR (open item cumulative balance) from the valuation 10 calculation (70,525 EUR in this example).

- **Amount in Group Currency.** This is the open item cumulative balance in Group Currency ($96,055.05 USD in this example).

- **Amount Valuated.** This is the Transaction Currency (72,610 EUR) translated into Group Currency ($96,193.72 USD) on the key date, less the translated Group Currency amount from "Type 10" valuation ($2,762.21 USD); $93,431.52 USD is the valuated amount in this example.

- **Old Difference.** This is the cumulative valuation adjustment that resulted from the most recent valuation.

- **New Difference.** This is the current cumulative valuation adjustment, which is the open item cumulative balance in Global Currency (96,055.05 USD), less the valuated amount ($93,431.52 USD) (First Local Currency translated to USD).

SAP Execution: Posting

```
CoCd Doc.no.    Document header text      Type  Pstg date  Curr. Text
Itm PK G/L acct   Text                                     Amount  Amt.in loc.cur.       LC2 amount

UK01 100000022  FC valuation SAPF100            02/28/2005 GBP
  1 40 230010      140000 - Valuation by 20050228          0.00           0.00           2,623.53
  2 50 140099      140000 - Valuation by 20050228          0.00           0.00           2,623.53

UK01 100000023  Reverse posting SAPF100         03/01/2005 GBP
  1 50 230010      140000 - Valuation by 20050228          0.00           0.00           2,623.53
  2 40 140099      140000 - Valuation by 20050228          0.00           0.00           2,623.53
```

© SAP AG, 2006

- **Local Currency Amount.** This is not relevant in this valuation method "Type 30."

- **Local Currency 2 Amount.** This is the original Group Currency ($96,055.05 USD) less the valuated amount ($93,431.52 USD).

- **Process Batch Session.** If a batch session was created, run transaction SM35 to process the batch session. Select "Process errors only," and Execute.

SAP Execution: Validation

In order to validate the results, select a few G/L accounts to analyze. Use the following steps to compare the revaluation from Transaction to Local Currency:

Step 1. Run SAP transaction code FBL3N for the open items on the key date for the same G/L accounts selected, or select a few to review. Exclude the amounts (Transaction Currency) where they are zero so you do not pick up adjustment amounts. Take the Transaction Currency and convert it to the Local Currency using the exchange rate for the key date being used.

Step 2. Take the original Local Currency (prior period) and the Local Currency amount calculated by the previous step and compare the SAP calculation, Exhibit 6.6.

> If foreign currency revaluation is run with multiple company codes and any of the G/L accounts being run in the same valuation mixed definitions between open item and non–open item, then SAP will use the specifications in this table and ignore any configuration in the previous table V-T030.

One Valuation Area	Transaction/ Document Currency		Local/ Functional Currency		Group/ Reporting Currency			Exchange Rates	
	Amount	Currency	Amount	Currency	Amount	Currency		GBP/EUR	EUR/USD
5-Jan	50,000.00	GBP	70,525.00	EUR	96,055.05	USD	M-Rate	1.4105	1.36200
31-Jan	50,000.00	GBP	72,105.00	EUR	94,068.18	USD	Spot-Rate	1.4421	1.30460
28-Feb	50,000.00	GBP	72,610.00	EUR	96,193.73	USD	Spot-Rate	1.4522	1.32480

Period 2	Transaction/ Document Currency		Local/ Functional Currency		Group/ Reporting Currency	
	Amount	Currency	Amount	Currency	Amount	Currency
2/28-reval 10	50,000.00	GBP	2,085.00	EUR	2,762.21	USD
2/28 cum.bal.	50,000.00	GBP		EUR	93,431.52	USD
2/28-CTA	50,000.00	GBP		EUR	−2,623.53	USD

Exhibit 6.6 Excel Calculation

154

	Transaction is Accessed via:
Via Menus	IMG → Financial Accounting → Accts Rec. & Accts Pay. → Business Transactions → Closing → Valuate → Foreign Currency Valuation → Define Depreciation Areas (Exhibit 6.8)
Via Transaction Code	SPRO

Exhibit 6.7   Access Sequence

UNIQUE CONFIGURATION

The valuation areas are defined here as in Exhibit 6.7. Exhibit 6.7 describes the menu path and transaction code, and Exhibit 6.8 shows it on the menu. Valuation areas are required with this valuation method. Valuation areas store the translated amounts in table BSIS. Valuation areas are freely definable, as in Exhibit 6.9.

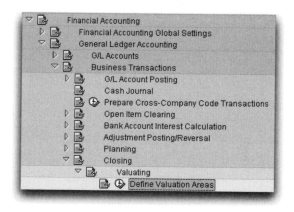

Exhibit 6.8   Menu Path

© SAP AG, 2006

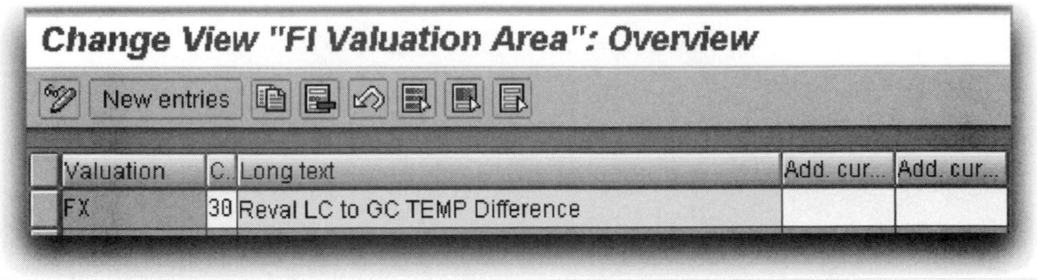

Change View "FI Valuation Area": Overview

	Valuation	C.	Long text	Add. cur..	Add. cur..
	FX	30	Reval LC to GC TEMP Difference		

- **FX.** FX is the only valuation area required for this method of revaluation. FX represents Group Currency, and is used for temporarily storing the first step (local to group translation difference) of the valuation in the FASB 52 tab. Separate account assignments on this valuation area are not required.

Exhibit 6.9   Define Valuation Areas

© SAP AG, 2006

7

COMMON REVALUATION CONFIGURATION

HIGHLIGHTS

- Define Local Currencies per Company Code
- Exchange Rate Types
- Valuation Methods
- Document Types
- Revaluation Account Assignments for Non–Open Item Accounts
- Revaluation Account Assignments for Open Item Accounts
- Translation
- Payment Program Translation Activation

DEFINE LOCAL CURRENCIES PER COMPANY CODE

The Local Currency of the company code is defined here as in Exhibit 7.3. Exhibit 7.1 describes the menu path and transaction code, and Exhibit 7.2 shows it on the menu. Additional currencies can be defined as Local Currency 2 and Local Currency 3, respectively. This area is key to setting up company codes and translation requirements correctly. Typically, the first Local Currency is set up as the country currency, and the second Local Currency is set up as the reporting/Group Currency.

	Transaction is Accessed via:
Via Menus	IMG → Financial Accounting → Financial Accounting Global Settings → Company Code → Multiple Currencies → Define Additional Local Currencies (Exhibit 7.2)
Via Transaction Code	SPRO

Exhibit 7.1 Access Sequence

If you change the settings on the source currency for the second and third local currencies, the values in BKPF-BASWx will become incorrect. Refer to SAP Note No. 335608 in the References at the end of the book.

In Exhibit 7.3, the second Local Currency settings are commonly used in the industry, with the exception of the "source currency," which can be set to either the Transaction Currency or the first Local Currency. If set to "2," the revaluation program takes the first Local Currency amount to calculate the amount in "Type 30." If set to "1," it uses the Transaction Currency as the basis for the revaluation 30 calculation. ours

The source currency is key to foreign currency valuation and should not be changed after postings have been made. Source currency equal to "1"

Exhibit 7.2 Menu Path
© SAP AG, 2006

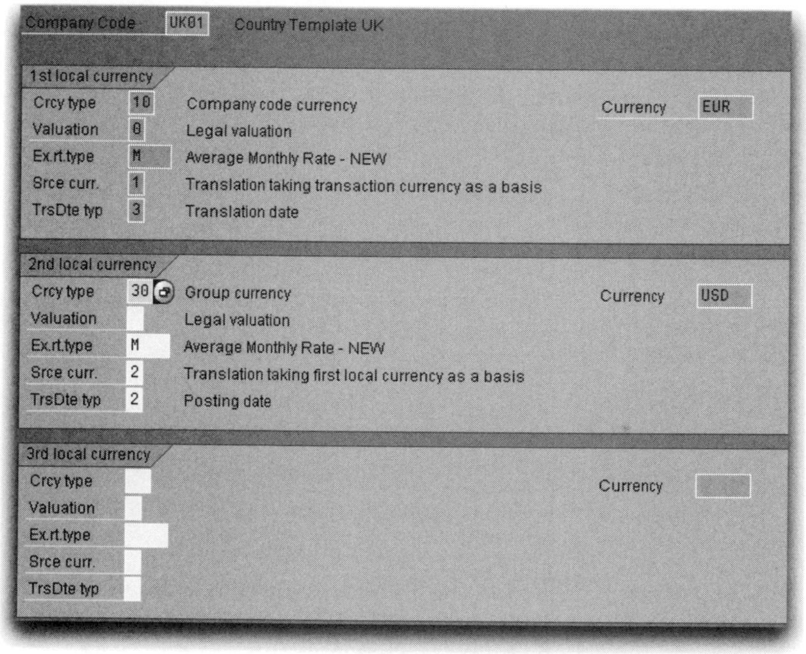

Exhibit 7.3 Company Code Currencies Defined
© SAP AG, 2006

takes the Transaction Currency as the basis of revaluation. Source currency equal to "2" takes the first Local Currency (valuated currency) as the basis.

EXCHANGE RATE TYPES

Exchange rate types are used in all currency revaluations, either directly, such as in the FASB 52 execution, or indirectly, through the configuration of the valuation method. They are set up in the IMG via Exhibit 7.4. Exhibit 7.4 describes the menu path and transaction code, and Exhibit 7.5 shows it on the menu. The exchange rate type is used specifically to identify the type of exchange rate in the TCURR table.

The exchange rate type is freely definable. "B" in Exhibit 7.6 is used in this example for the spot rate. More specific settings are available if required, such as the reference currency and buying/selling currency rates.

	Transaction is Accessed via:
Via Menus	IMG → General Settings → Currencies → Check Exchange Rate Types (Exhibit 7.5)
Via Transaction Code	SPRO

Exhibit 7.4   Access Sequence

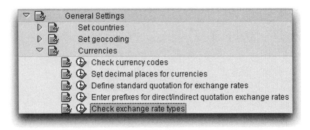

Exhibit 7.5   Menu Path
© SAP AG, 2006

DEFINE VALUATION METHODS

Valuation methods group a set of instructions for the valuation execution at month end. The detail and posting instructions for the valuation are defined in the IMG via Exhibit 7.7. Exhibit 7.7 describes the menu path and transaction code, and Exhibit 7.8 shows it on the menu. The valuation method is a specific parameter identified in the revaluation run.

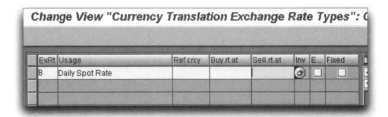

Exhibit 7.6   Exchange Rate Type Configuration
© SAP AG, 2006

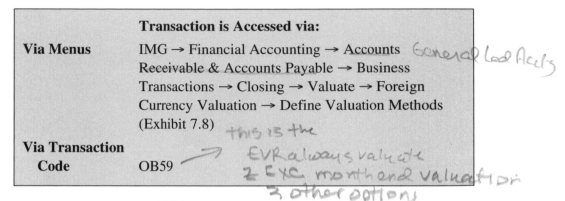

	Transaction is Accessed via:
Via Menus	IMG → Financial Accounting → Accounts Receivable & Accounts Payable → Business Transactions → Closing → Valuate → Foreign Currency Valuation → Define Valuation Methods (Exhibit 7.8)
Via Transaction Code	OB59

Handwritten notes: General Led Accts

Handwritten notes: this is the → EVR always valuate 2 Exc month end valuation 3 other options

Exhibit 7.7   Access Sequence

In order to be able to reverse revaluation runs without having to manually reverse the journal entries, set up a unique valuation method as the "Reset selected," "always valuate." Use this valuation method and select the "balance sheet prep" indicator when executing the reversal run. Refer to SAP Note No. 545032 in the References for more information.

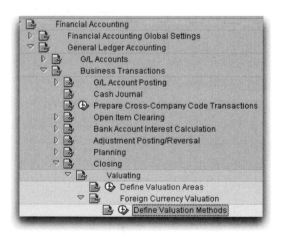

Exhibit 7.8   Menu Path

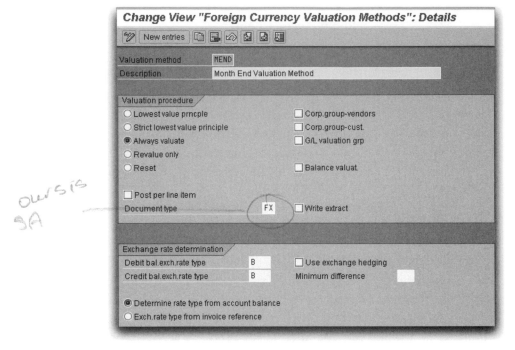

Exhibit 7.9   Valuation Methods Defined
© SAP AG, 2006

Valuation methods provide the definition of how to run currency revaluation. Detailed settings are customizable, and specific field settings are shown in Exhibit 7.9. An explanation of each option in the exhibit follows:

- **Lowest Value Principle.** If selected, Local Currency valuation is only displayed if it is a loss (difference between the Local Currency amount and the valuated amount is negative).

- **Strict Lowest Value Principle.** If selected, Local Currency valuation is only displayed if its loss is greater than the previous valuation entries.

- **Always Valuate.** If selected, revaluations are always executed and posted.

- **Revalue Only.** If selected, revaluations (increases/gains), not devaluations (decreases/losses), will occur.

- **Reset (Valuation Run).** If selected, open items are valuated at the acquisition price, account determination is reversed, old valuation method is reset, and the valuation difference is set to zero. This is commonly used when setting up a valuation method to reverse revaluation runs.

- **Corp Group-Vendors/Customers.** G/L accounts are valuated according to the valuation group, and customer and vendor accounts are valuated according to the customer and vendor group key in the customer/vendor master records.

- **G/L Valuation Group.** If selected, open items are balanced per account/group and currency. If not selected, open items are summarized and valuated per reference number, and if no reference number exists, then each line item is valuated individually.

- **Balance Valuation.** If not selected (which is more common), open items are summarized and valuated individually by reference number (if it exists). If selected, open items are summarized, valued, and balanced by account, group, and currency.

- **Post per Line Item.** If selected, a line item per valued item is posted in the valuation postings and the adjustment account; otherwise, it is posted in summarized form.

- **Write Extract.** If selected, the revaluation run via F.05 must have a batch session name. Information is stored in this file for each valuated line item. Normally, this is not selected unless there is a non-SAP application need for the extracted file.

- **Document Type.** See configuration in the common area to configure the settings for a valuation document type. Generally, the document type assigned here would be different from the common document types used in normal transaction postings. This will allow for easier account analysis. $\rightarrow$ monthly daily average etc

- **Debit Balance Exchange Rate Type.** The exchange rate type is used for valuation of foreign currency items with a positive balance.

- **Credit Balance Exchange Rate Type.** The exchange rate type is used for valuation of foreign currency items with a negative balance.

- **Determine Exchange Rate Type from Account Balance.** The currency valuation is determined based on the account balance in the relevant currency.

- **Exchange Rate Type from Invoice Reference.** The currency valuation is determined based on the balance per invoice reference number.

- **Use Exchange Hedging.** If selected, items are valuated at the hedged exchange rate.

- **Minimum Difference for Display in Foreign Currency Valuation.** This field indicator allows one to suppress currency rounding differences up to the selected amount for hedged or fixed exchange rate calculations.

DEFINE DOCUMENT TYPES FOR CURRENCY REVALUATION

Document types provide the ability to uniquely identify postings of a particular type (e.g., foreign currency revaluation postings). They are defined in the SAP IMG through Exhibit 7.10. Exhibit 7.10 describes the menu path and transaction code, and Exhibit 7.11 shows it on the menu. They provide the means to uniquely define a number range, a document type to reverse the postings on, and the allowed posting account types (e.g., G/L accounts, vendors, customers, and fixed assets).

It is recommended to create a document type, such as in Exhibit 7.12, that is unique for foreign currency postings. This allows you to quickly view these postings when viewing multiple documents.

The currency revaluation document type can be set up as shown in Exhibit 7.12.

Some of the key settings for the document type are defined as follows. Not all fields are discussed in this section.

	Transaction is Accessed via:
Via Menus	IMG → Financial Accounting → Financial Accounting Global Settings → Document → Document Header → Define Document Types (Exhibit 7.11)
Via Transaction Code	OBA7

Exhibit 7.10   Access Sequence

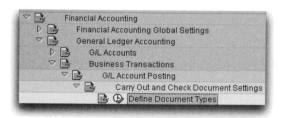

Exhibit 7.11 Menu Path

© SAP AG, 2006

- **Document Type.** The unique two-character document identifier to be used for posting currency valuation adjustments. This is defined in the valuation method used in currency revaluation.

- **Number Range.** Select the number range from those set up for accounting documents. The range used can be the same as for most of the

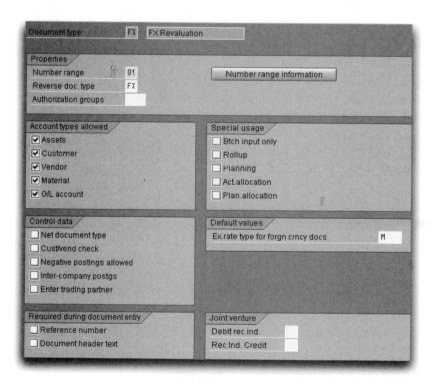

Exhibit 7.12 Revaluation Document Type

© SAP AG, 2006

accounting documents. The document type will be the unique identifier for these transactions.

- **Reverse Document Type.** The document identifier to be used for posting reversals of documents assigned the primary document type. This can be the same identifier as used for the primary document.

- **Account Types Allowed.** This indicates the type of accounts to which this document type can post.

REVALUATION ACCOUNT ASSIGNMENTS

Three tables can be configured for foreign currency revaluation. The following two are relevant to the revaluation method foreign currency revaluation without valuation areas. The third table is relevant only to valuation area usage and is covered as unique configuration within the respective chapter. All A/P, A/R, and all accounts that receive postings in a foreign currency must be configured in one of these two tables in order to be able to run revaluation. If the configuration does not exist for an account and SAP is calculating a realized Gain/Loss posting, the result will be a hard error. If the configuration does not exist and revaluation is run, SAP will generate a batch input session. This session will need to be processed, with corrections manually entered, to complete the postings.

Non–Open Item G/L Accounts (Table T030S)

This table is used for foreign currency revaluation account assignments for non–open item G/L accounts. This table requires the configuration and usage of Exchange Rate (E/R) difference keys on the G/L master records. Exchange Rate differences are posted to adjustment accounts only.

> If no entries exist in the SAP table T030S, then SAP searches the next table (V-T030H) for the correct account assignments. Refer to SAP Note No. 315155 and SAP Note No. 548946 in the References for more information on the order that SAP uses to search these tables to find the account assignments.

- Open Item G/L Accounts (table V-T030H). This table is used for the foreign currency revaluation account assignments for open item G/L accounts. Non–open item accounts can be configured in this table too.

> If foreign currency revaluation is run with multiple company codes and any of the G/L accounts being run have mixed definitions between open item and non–open item, SAP will use the specifications in this table and ignore any configuration in the previous table V-T030S (refer to SAP Note No. 312884 in the References for more information or instructions on how to change this default setting).

ACCOUNT ASSIGNMENTS FOR VALUATION: NON–OPEN ITEMS (V-T030S)

Non–open items that manage foreign currencies can be configured for revaluation in table V-T030S. This method of configuring (Exhibit 7.13) non–open item accounts was required in earlier releases of SAP, but in later releases of SAP, both non–open item and open item accounts can be configured in the same area/table (V-T030S). Exhibit 7.13 describes the menu path and transaction code, and Exhibit 7.14 shows it on the menu.

The table in Exhibit 7.15 allows for configuring non–open items and open item accounts. Select KDB to configure non–open item accounts.

	Transaction is Accessed via:
Via Menus	IMG → Financial Accounting → Accts Rec. & Accts Pay. → Business Transactions → Closing → Valuate → Foreign Currency Valuation → Prepare Automatic Posting for Foreign Currency Valuation (Exhibit 7.14)
Via Transaction Code	OBA1

Exhibit 7.13 Access Sequence

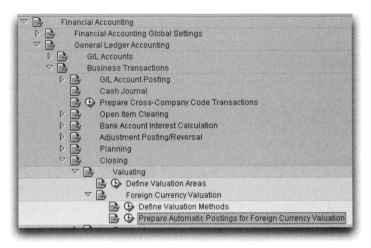

Exhibit 7.14   Menu Path

© SAP AG, 2006

The exchange rate field is freely definable in Exhibit 7.16. This enables postings for non–open items by assigning the exchange rate field on the G/L account. Exhibit 7.17 describes the menu path and transaction code, and Exhibit 7.18 shows it on the menu. In this example, G/L accounts assigned E/R key "USD" will have gains/losses posted to G/L account 230000.

> The E/R key is assigned to the G/L account in the G/L account master record.

Group	FWA	Exchange rate differences	

Procedures		
Description	Transactn	Account determ.
Exch.rate diff. in forgn.curr.balances	KDB	✓
Exchange rate difference in open items	KDF	✓
Payment difference for altern.currency	KDW	✓
Payment diff.for altern.curr.(offset)	KDZ	✓
Internal currencies rounding differences	RDF	✓

Exhibit 7.15   Exchange Rate Difference Transaction KDB

© SAP AG, 2006

| Chart of accounts | INT | Chart of accounts - international |
| Transaction | KDB | Exch.rate diff. in forgn.curr.balances |

Account assignment

Exchange r...	Expense a...	E/R gains ...	Roll.val.exp.	Roll.val.rev.
	230000	280000		
FRF	230000	280000		
USD	230000	280000		

Exhibit 7.16 Exchange Rate Difference Using Exchange Rate Key

	Transaction is Accessed via:
Via Menus	IMG → Financial Accounting → Accounts Receivable & Accounts Payable → Business Transactions → Closing → Valuate → Foreign Currency Valuation → Prepare Automatic Posting for Foreign Currency Valuation (Exhibit 7.18)
Via Transaction Code	OBA1

Exhibit 7.17 Access Sequence

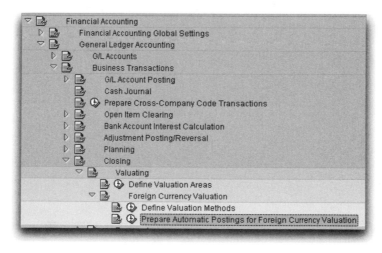

Exhibit 7.18 Menu Path

ACCOUNT ASSIGNMENTS FOR VALUATION: OPEN ITEMS (V-T030H)

This table (V-T030H) should be maintained if postings are made in a foreign Transaction Currency to open item managed balance sheet accounts or reconciliation accounts.

Non–open item managed accounts can also be maintained in this table as long as they are not maintained in V-T030S.

The table in Exhibit 7.19 allows for configuring non–open items and open item accounts. Select KDF to configure open item accounts.

Header Information

Foreign currency account assignments are not company code specific, but they can be controlled by the currency and currency type. Normally, a blank Currency Type and Currency "Type 30" are the two setups used for each G/L account being revaluated. A blank Currency Type will be used for all Currency Types not specifically identified, as in Exhibit 7.20.

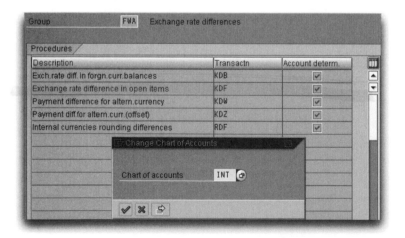

Exhibit 7.19   Exchange Rate Differences (transaction KDF)

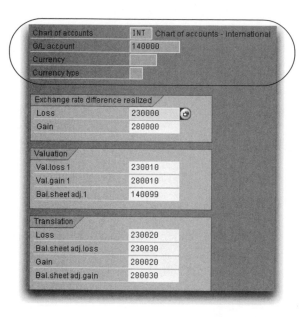

- **G/L Account.** This is the balance sheet account in which foreign currencies are managed and revaluated.

- **Currency.** If left blank, this configuration is used for all valuations. The Currency field can also be used to more selectively configure G/L account assignments. It is important to note that SAP looks at the Transaction Currency, not the Local Currency, on the posting when this field is uniquely identified, regardless of how currency configuration is defined.

- **Currency Type.** If left blank, this configuration is used for all the revaluations not otherwise specified. Default account assignments can be set per currency type valuations. "Type 10" revaluation (transaction to Local Currency) can designate one set of account assignments and "Type 30" revaluation (transaction to Group Currency) can designate another.

Exhibit 7.20   Maintain Account Assignments
© SAP AG, 2006

Exchange Rate Difference Realized

Realized Gain/Loss postings occur in SAP when the postings are cleared in open item managed accounts. Exhibit 7.21 shows where the G/L accounts are configured for posting the Gains/Losses.

When the original posting is cleared in SAP, the realized Gain/Loss posting is calculated by SAP by taking the original posting Transaction Currency and translating it to Local Currency on the clearing translation date. SAP

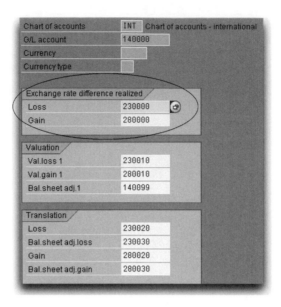

- **Realized Loss G/L.** Account for losses from realized exhange rate fluctuations (posted when clearing open items in foreign currency).

- **Realized Gain G/L.** Account for gains from realized exchange rate fluctuations (posted when clearing open items in foreign currency).

- **Valuation.** These are the accounts that the unrealized Gain/Losses are posted to when foreign currency revaluation is executed, Exhibit 7.22. They become realized when they are cleared.

Exhibit 7.21   Realized Exchange Rate Gain/Loss Accounts

© SAP AG, 2006

then posts the difference from the original posting that remains unchanged and the newly calculated value as the realized Gain/Loss. At the same time, SAP does the same type of translation from Transaction Currency to Group Currency and posts that difference as realized Gain/Loss.

During some postings, it may appear that the system is posting a zero amount, realized Gain/Loss posting. SAP will display the line item if the Gain/Loss is in a different currency (Document, Local, or Group). Change the currency display to view the amount in the currency that was translated.

Chart of accounts	INT	Chart of accounts - international
G/L account	140000	
Currency		
Currency type		

Exchange rate difference realized

Loss	230000	
Gain	280000	

Valuation

Val.loss 1	230010
Val.gain 1	280010
Bal.sheet adj.1	140099

Translation

Loss	230020
Bal.sheet adj.loss	230030
Gain	280020
Bal.sheet adj.gain	280030

- **Valuation Loss.** Account for losses from the foreign currency valuation of open items.
- **Valuation Gain.** Account for gains from the foreign currency valuation of open items.
- **Balance Sheet Adjustment.** The Balance Sheet Adjustment Account is the account to which the receivables and/or payables adjustment are posted during the foreign currency valuation of open items. If the G/L account is a reconciliation account, this must be a different G/L account that allows direct postings (as reconciliation accounts do not allow direct postings). In general, it is recommended that the B/S accounts be separate accounts from the G/L account, as the gain/loss postings from revaluation 10 could get picked up for revaluation again during revaluation 30 (depending on the version and patch level of SAP).

Exhibit 7.22   Valuation Gain/Loss and Balance Sheet Adjustment Accounts
© SAP AG, 2006

Realized Gain/Loss postings can also occur during foreign currency intercompany postings, including but not limited to stock transports that involve foreign currency values.

VALUATION

These are the accounts that the unrealized Gain/Losses are posted to when foreign currency revaluation is executed. They become realized when cleared.

If you do use the same B/S adjustment account as the G/L account being revaluated, and the second source currency is set to "2," to take the first Local Currency amounts, then enter a selection parameter to exclude postings with transaction currencies equal to zero and the revaluated Gain/Loss postings will be ignored.

TRANSLATION

Exhibit 7.23 determines whether translation Gains/Losses are posted during clearing foreign currency open item processing (such as during payment processing). Translations occur if the items to be cleared already have been revaluated via F.05 and unrealized Gains/Losses have been posted. The valuation difference is posted to a separate translation account and the offset to a clearing account.

INCOMING PAYMENTS: TRANSLATION POSTING ACTIVATION

This configuration in Exhibit 7.24 determines whether translation Gains/Losses are posted during clearing of foreign currency open items, and Exhibit 7.25 shows where it is on the menu. Translations are posted if the item being cleared has been revaluated during periodic currency revaluation.

To enable translations, select the indicator (Exhibit 7.26) for the relevant company codes.

PAYMENT PROGRAM TRANSLATION ACTIVATION

This setting (Exhibit 7.27) determines whether translation Gains/Losses are posted during clearing of foreign currency open items, and Exhibit 7.28 shows it on the menu. Translations are posted if the item being cleared has been revaluated during periodic currency revaluation.

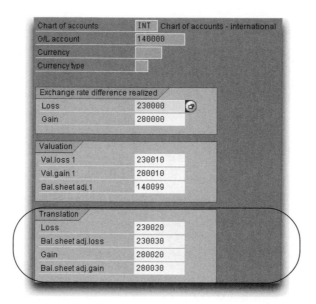

- **Translation Loss.** This is the posting account for foreign currency translation losses as defined previously. This account can be the same as or different from the gains account.

- **Balance Sheet Adjustment Loss.** Offset clearning posting to the translation loss posting. This account can be the same as or different from the balance sheet adjustment gain account.

- **Translation Gain.** Posting account for foreign currency translation gains as defined above. This account can be the same as or different from the loss account.

- **Balance Sheet Adjustment Gain.** Offset clearing posting to the translation gain posting. This account can be the same as or different from the balance sheet adjustment loss account.

Exhibit 7.23   Translation Gain/Loss and Balance Sheet Adjustment Accounts

© SAP AG, 2006

	Transaction is Accessed via:
Via Menus	IMG → Financial Accounting → Accts Rec. & Accts Pay. → Business Transactions → Incoming Payments → Incoming Payments Global Settings → Enable Translation Posting (Exhibit 7.25)
Via Transaction Code	SPRO

Exhibit 7.24   Access Sequence

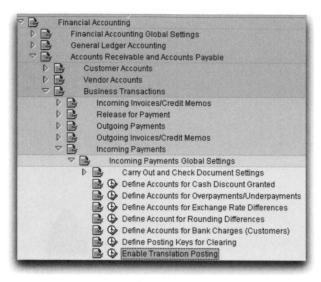

Exhibit 7.25   Menu Path

© SAP AG, 2006

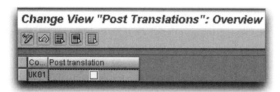

Exhibit 7.26   Post Translations

© SAP AG, 2006

	Transaction is Accessed via:
Via Menus	IMG → Financial Accounting → Accts Rec. & Accts Pay. → Business Transactions → Outgoing Payments → Automatic Outgoing Payments → Payment Method/Bank Selection for Payment Program → Set up Paying Company Codes for Payment Transactions (Exhibit 7.28)
Via Transaction Code	

Exhibit 7.27   Access Sequence

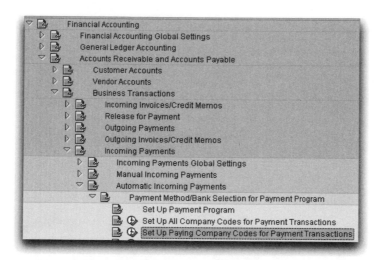

Exhibit 7.28 Menu Path
© SAP AG, 2006

Exchange Rate Differences during Payment Processing

This indicator (Exhibit 7.29) determines whether exchange rate differences are to be posted by the payment program. If the indicator is selected, exchange rate differences are not calculated. The Local Currency amount would represent the total Local Currencies from the cleared items (not the foreign currency translation). If the indicator is not set, the differences are calculated from the original posting and from the clearing/payment posting for foreign currencies using the exchange rate on the payment program translation date.

Exchange Rate Indicator

Set the "No Exchange Rate Differences" indicator to post translation Gains/ Losses during open item clearing.

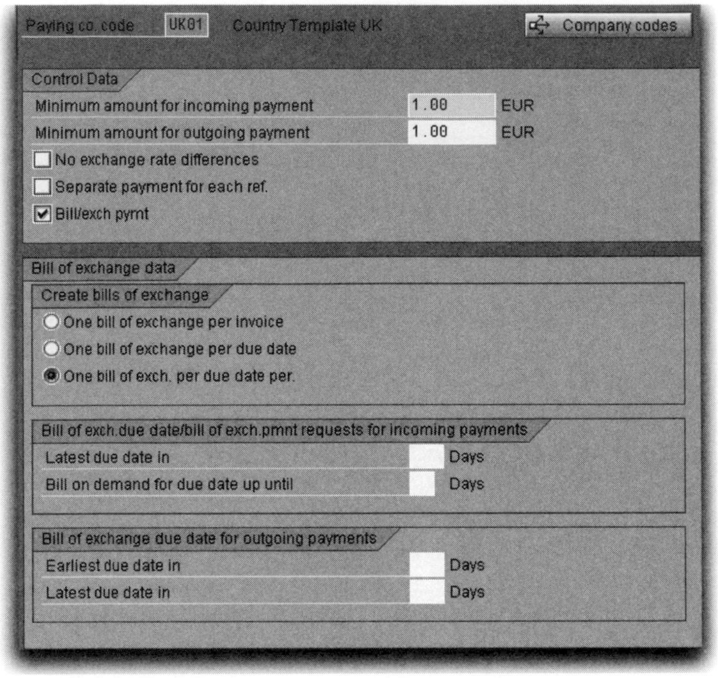

Exhibit 7.29 Payment Program Post Translations

© SAP AG, 2006

8

VALUATION VARIANT SETUP

HIGHLIGHTS

- Revaluation List Variant
- Revaluation Posting Variant

Custom variants are a way to display reports or execution outputs and selectively identify key fields that are important to the evaluation. Custom variants can be set up for the currency valuation calculations and the currency valuation postings. The currency valuation calculation variant can be set up and selected on the currency revaluation tab. The postings variant cannot be saved to display automatically and must be reselected for each valuation and display of the postings. The samples created here can be adjusted for more custom requirements.

LIST/CALCULATION VARIANT

The List/Calculation variant shows the values that are used in the currency valuation calculations. The default SAP display has minimal fields displayed. The variant in Exhibit 8.1 allows for a one-screen viewing of the critical fields. This can be modified for a more custom view if desired. To set up the

179

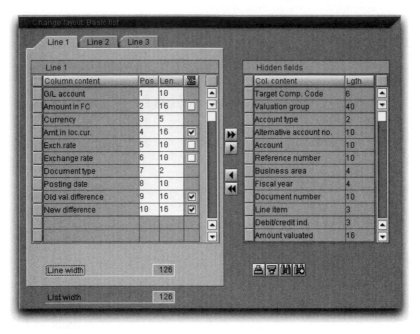

Exhibit 8.1   Set up the List Variant "/FXREVALUE" Example
© SAP AG, 2006

display variant for currency valuation calculations, select the Line 1 Tab, as in Exhibit 8.1, and set up the indicators as shown. Setup the sort order as shown in Exhibit 8.2.

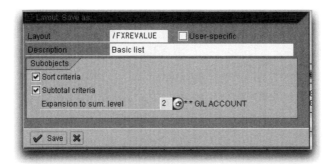

Exhibit 8.2   Save the List Variant Sort Order Example
© SAP AG, 2006

POSTING VARIANT

The posting variant shows how the postings will be made in SAP. If account assignment errors occur, they will be visible on this display. The default SAP display has all fields available displayed and requires scrolling to the right to view all fields. The variant in Exhibit 8.3 allows for a one-screen viewing of the critical fields. This can be modified for a more custom view if desired. To set up the posting variant to view three currencies, select the Header Tab and the Line 1 tab, as in Exhibit 8.3.

Select the Position Tab and then the Line 1 tab and select the fields as displayed in Exhibit 8.4.

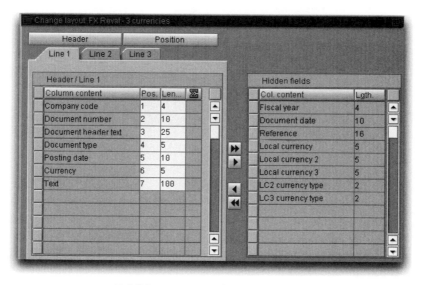

Exhibit 8.3 Header Tab Setup

© SAP AG, 2006

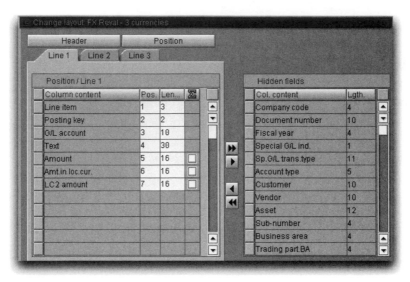

Exhibit 8.4 Position Tab Setup

© SAP AG, 2006

Save the variant as displayed in Exhibit 8.5.

Exhibit 8.5 Position Tab Setup

© SAP AG, 2006

APPENDIX

Transaction Codes (T-Codes)

OC41	Define/Enter Exchange Rates
OBA1	Configure Automatic Postings for Foreign Currency Valuation
OBYC	Configure Inventory Valuation Account Assignments
OBY6	Configure Global Company Code Setup
OBYY	Configure Account for Exchange Rate Difference Postings (not normally for U.S. companies)
OB59	Configure Valuation Methods
OBA7	Configure Document types
F.05	Currency Revaluation Execution
F.13	G/L Clearing

> now FQ6N ?

References: SAP OSS Note

SAP Note No. 441333   SAPF100 Logic with GR/IR accounts
11.03.2005

SAP Note No. 87538   SAPF100 - posting system
03.09.2004

SAP Note No. 315155   Account determination for valuation area
31.08.2004

SAP Note No. 335608   Source Currency Settings

SAP Note No. 448306   FASB52 in FI with Release 4.6C
31.08.2004

SAP Note No. 545032   FAQ: SAPF100 Reversing "Balance Sheet Prep."
03.09.2004

SAP Note No. 548946   FAQ: SAPF100 Account Determination
03.09.2004

SAP Note No. 692693   SAPF100: Performance improvement w/ BDIFF update
02.11.2004

SAP Note No. 312884   RFSBEW00: Changed account determination
22.09.2004

GLOSSARY

Conversion

The exchange of one currency for another.

Cumulative Translation Adjustment (CTA)

The exchange rate movement Gain/Loss between the Local Currency and the Group Currency exchange rates. Posted to a G/L account within shareholder's equity.

Currency, Document

The currency in which transactions take place. Also known as *Transactional Currency* or *Foreign Currency*.

Currency, Foreign

The currencies in which transactions take place that are different from the Local Currency. Also known as *Transactional Currency* or *Document Currency*.

Currency, Functional

The currency of the primary environment in which the entity operates, generates or expends cash. Also known as *Local Currency*.

Currency, Group

The reporting currency of the enterprise. Also referred to as *Local Currency 2* and *Parallel Currency*.

Currency, Local

The currency of the particular company code and country. Also known as the *Functional Currency*.

Currency, Local 2

The reporting currency of the enterprise. Also referred to as *Group Currency* and *Parallel Local Currency*.

Currency, Parallel

The reporting currency of the enterprise. Also referred to as *Group Currency* and *Local Currency 2*.

Currency, Reporting

The currency in which financial statements are prepared.

Currency, Transactional

The currency in which transactions take place. Also known as *Document Currency* or *Foreign Currency*.

Exchange Rate

The exchange rate is the rate at which one unit of a currency can be exchanged for (converted into) another currency on a particular date.

FASB

Financial Accounting Standards Board.

FASB 52

Financial Accounting Standards Board—document 52.

Foreign Currency

A currency other than the Local Currency. Also known as *Functional Currency* or *Transactional Currency* of an entity.

Foreign Currency Transactions

Occur when an item is transacted in a foreign currency.

Revaluation "type 10"

Differences arising from the document to Local Currency revaluation. Calculated as the difference between the Local Currency value on the original posting date and on the current key revaluation date. Differences are posted to a P&L account.

Revaluation "type 10" with translation

Includes revaluation "type 10" and another posting (on the same line item) that translates the Gain/Loss from Local Currency to Group Currency based on the fluctuation of the exchange rate.

Revaluation "type 30" (CTA, Currency Translation Adjustment)

Differences arising from the Local to Group Currency revaluation. Calculated as the difference between the Group Currency value on the original posting date and on the current key revaluation date (Local Currency amount times the FX exchange rate Gain/Loss differences).

Transaction Date

The date on which a transaction is recorded.

GLOSSARY

Transaction Gain/Losses

Result from a change in exchange rates on transactions that occur in nonlocal currencies. It represents an increase or decrease in the transaction's original value based on the current exchange rate.

Translation

The translation between the Local Currency and the Group Currency for reporting purposes.

Translation Adjustments

Result from the process of translating financial statements from Functional to Reporting currency.

INDEX

INDEX